A Gift of Love
To

Sam Bartlett

May God Bless your
work. And may you
enjoy this Book

March
'87

Affectionately

Don F Hamilton

MEGA TRUTH

THE CHURCH IN THE AGE OF INFORMATION

DAVID McKENNA

Here's Life Publishers

Published by
HERE'S LIFE PUBLISHERS, INC.
P.O. Box 1576
San Bernardino, California 92402

HLP Product No. 951392
©1986, David L. McKenna

Library of Congress Cataloging-in-Publication Data

McKenna, David L. (David Loren), 1929-
    Megatruth : the church in the age of information.

    Bibliography: p.
    Includes index.
    1. Christianity — 20th century. 2. Naisbitt, John.
Megatrends. 3. Social indicators — United States.
4. Social prediction — United States. 5. United States —
Social conditions — 1980-   . I. Title.
BR481.M24   1986   261.1   86-12153
ISBN 0-89840-136-4

FOR MORE INFORMATION, WRITE:

L.I.F.E. — P.O. Box A399, Sydney South 2000, Australia
Campus Crusade for Christ of Canada — Box 300, Vancouver, B.C. V6C 2X3, Canada
Campus Crusade for Christ — 103 Friar Street, Reading RG1 1EP, Berkshire, England
Lay Institute for Evangelism — P.O. Box 8786, Auckland 3, New Zealand
Great Commission Movement of Nigeria — P.O. Box 500, Jos, Plateau State Nigeria, West Africa
Campus Crusade for Christ International — Arrowhead Springs, San Bernardino, CA 92414, U.S.A.

To my sons
Doug and Rob,
to my sons-in-law
Ed and Scott,
who challenge my ideas,
groan at my jokes,
and keep me young

CONTENTS

Acknowledgments 9

INTRODUCTION

Chapter 1-Megatrends,
    Megashifts, and MegaTruth 13

PART 1
CRISIS
OF TRUTH

Chapter 2-Reading the Signs
    of the Times 21
Chapter 3-Living in a
    Time of Parenthesis 35
Chapter 4-Anticipating the
    Age of Information 49

PART 2
MEANING
OF MEGATRUTH

Chapter 5-The Spirit of Truth 57
Chapter 6-The Synthesizing
    Spirit 65
Chapter 7-The Norming Spirit 73
Chapter 8-The Futuring Spirit 83
Chapter 9-The Engaging Spirit 89

PART 3
MEGATRUTH
FOR MEGATRENDS

Chapter 10-Hi/Touch for Our
    Relationships 97
Chapter 11-Hi/Test for Our
    Stewardship 115
Chapter 12-Hi/Energy for Our
    Organizations 127
Chapter 13-Hi/Net for Our
    Evangelism 147
Chapter 14-Hi/Power for Our
    Leadership 161
Chapter 15-Hi/Tone for Our
    Witness 175

CONCLUSION

Chapter 16-A Tract for
    Our Times 195

Notes 203
Bibliography 209

Acknowledgments

I never intended to write a book.

At the meeting of the National Association of Evangelicals in Los Angeles in 1984, I gave a luncheon address on the subject, "Hi/Truth Teaching in a Hi/Tech World." Immediately afterward, Les Stobbe introduced himself with the invitation, "Will you write a book?" The idea piqued my interest, but I answered no because of other writing and fund-raising commitments. Les persisted. A letter repeating the invitation came and a series of telephone calls followed. Like the importunate man knocking on the door in the middle of the night in Jesus' parable, Les pressed his case and got his book. Ernest Hemingway said the greatest inspiration for his writing was the publisher's deadline. Thanks to Les Stobbe, I can now expand the adage of inspiration to include the publisher's persistence.

To this day I don't know how or when I wrote the book. The fall of 1985 is a time of shadows which I barely remember. Someplace, in the bits and pieces of early morning, long weekends, and mini-vacations, I wrote and wrote. Those who knew me in my younger days will notice a new gap in my discretionary time for writing. No longer do I achieve high productivity between midnight and dawn. At best, I use the evening hours to read for new ideas and jog for a new perspective that will guide my writing the next day. Age shows most, however, with my confession that I also suffered insomnia from time to time and ended up scratching notes on a yellow pad which made no sense in the morning.

Through it all, however, I experienced an engagement with the mind of Christ through the work of the Holy Spirit which I have never known before. Early on I decided that I could not call the church to claim Jesus' promise that He would send us the Spirit of Truth to "show us things to come" unless I submitted myself and especially my mind to His thoughts and His Spirit. Therefore, if the book has a turning point, it is the

9

.oment when I recognized that we know the Truth by spiritual engagement with Truth itself. Only out of this relationship with the indwelling Spirit dare we breathe the bold word "MegaTruth." Any shred of arrogance is stripped away by the knowledge that the word we speak or the Truth we see is not our own. It is only through the clear lens of Christ's revelation and the keen focus of the Spirit's teaching that we dare to write or speak about things to come. Therefore with humility and gratitude, I present these thoughts as a learning and growing student of the Spirit of Truth.

As always, this book is not my own. It belongs to my Seminary, our trustees, faculty, students, and alumni, with the prayer that it may advance our mission. It belongs to my readers for their criticism and nurture. It belongs to my wife, Janet, and our family, as part of their heritage. It belongs to my president's staff, Sheila Lovell and Lois Mulcahy, who share in the pride of its production. It belongs most of all to my Christ, to be used for His glory.

INTRODUCTION

MEGATRENDS, MEGASHIFTS, AND MEGATRUTH

1.

Megatrends, Megashifts, and MegaTruth

What book is on more library shelves in the United States than any other volume including any version of the Bible or any single work of Shakespeare?

What book set a record for sixty straight weeks on the *New York Times* best-seller list?

What book is acclaimed as a "field guide to the future" and "a road map to the twenty-first century"?

To each question, the answer is *Megatrends.*[1] Written by John Naisbitt, *Megatrends* is the nation's best-seller for the 1980s, selling multimillions of copies and vaulting its author from the edge of bankruptcy onto the dizzying heights of the rich and the famous. Even today, Naisbitt can command thousands of dollars for a single lecture and is guaranteed million-dollar sales for anything he writes.

Scholars may question Naisbitt's methods of research, the soundness of his premises, and the sweep of his observations, but no one can dispute the impact of the book upon the American mind. *Megatrends* is a book that will not go away. Only its

13

companion best-seller, *In Search of Excellence,* can compete with *Megatrends* as the most-quoted book of the 1980s. Its use ranges from a corporate guide for strategic planning to a neighborhood selection for a coffee-cup discussion group.

Why the continuing demand for *Megatrends?* Is it the punchy title that attracts our attention? Is our curiosity piqued by the intriguing subtitle, "Ten New Directions Transforming Our Lives"? Is it the jubilant ending meant to allay our fears about a Hi/Tech future? Or is it the author's fundamental thesis that we are in a "time of parenthesis" between two eras of human civilization?[2] On the back side of the parenthesis is the Age of Industry, which took over from the Age of Agriculture in the eighteenth century and came to its peak in the first half of the twentieth century. On the front edge of the parenthesis is what Naisbitt calls the forthcoming Age of Information which is, even now, coming into its own and making the Age of Industry obsolete.

Signs of the dawning Age of Information are all around us, says Naisbitt:

- 52 percent of our gross national product is spent in the communication industries.

- 60 percent of all jobs are in information-related fields.

- High-tech industries centering around silicon chips, microprocessors and computer software are the growth and glamor industries of the nation.

- Silicon Valley in California is said to have more brainpower in one place than Florence, Italy, at the time of the Renaissance.

Our minds begin to boggle when we try to envision the impact of high technology upon our way of life:

What will it be like when ideas, not coal, oil, gas or uranium become the primary fuel for our growth industries?

What will it be like when information is mass-produced for public consumption just as we have mass-produced cars and canned goods in the past?

What will it be like when power is defined not by money in the hands of a few, but by information in the hands of many?

MEGATRENDS TELLS US THAT EVERY AREA OF OUR LIVES WILL BE PROFOUNDLY AFFECTED.

As electronic circuitry takes over more and more in our lives, we will desperately seek the touch of human relationships.

As information is speeded around the world, we will truly become an interdependent global village.

It is predicted that as people are given more and more information, the power of old political parties will give way to networks of special interest.

With more information, people will challenge the political system by initiative and referendum rather than remain passive observers of the political process.

And this is just the beginning. According to Naisbitt, under the impact of information we will

turn from government help to self-help;

move south and west to the land of the silicon chip;

make computer language an educational requirement;

find a whole new world of options waiting for us in jobs, entertainment, food, family and even religion.

Perhaps *Time* magazine took a prophetic stance by featuring the computer as The Man of the Year for 1983. Certainly, high technology as represented by the computer is setting the theme and striking the tone for the remaining years of this decade and years to come.

But what is the spiritual meaning of *Megatrends?* We have been so enamored with the dramatic optimism of the book that we have failed to apply the discerning mind to its content. Hidden beneath the trend lines are some philosophical/spiritual assumptions that cannot be ignored. For instance, as the best-seller of the 1980s, Naisbitt's *Megatrends* replaces Hal Lindsey's *The Late Great Planet Earth,* which was the best-seller among all books for the 1970s. They represent two opposite poles in perspective. Lindsey comes to his writing as a Christian with a fundamentalist and dispensational mindset. Naisbitt, however, is a leading advocate of the New Age philosophy with its humanistic foundations, evolutionary thesis and cultic identity. Their attitudes are equally opposite. Lindsey closes his book with these words:

> The time is short.
>
> In the early centuries, the Christians had a word for greeting and departing; it was the word "maranatha," which means, "the Lord is coming soon." We can think of no better way with which to say goodbye —

MARANATHA![3]

Naisbitt, however, leaves us with the hope-filled shout,

My God, what a fantastic time to be alive!

If best-selling books signal the hopes and fears of a nation, the swing from Lindsey in the '70s to Naisbitt in the '80s is a "megashift" in our view of the future. Is the difference explained simply as the cycle of history? Perhaps after the earthshaking events of Dallas, My Lai, Woodstock, Kent State and Watergate, Lindsey's book expressed our national malaise, purged our soul, and set us on the search for new hope, which we found in *Megatrends*. Or is the difference political? At the same time that we downplay the power of the president, we realize that Nixon, Ford, Carter and Reagan are symbols of our shift from dark gloom to bright hope. Or was it the "born-again" movement of the 1970s that made the difference? Perhaps there is a critical mass of redeemed people who have turned the prevailing tone of the nation from despair to hope. If so, the perspective of time may well show us that we are witnessing a third Great Awakening in American history.

Whatever the reason for the change in the American mood, we must take *Megatrends* seriously and ask,

WHAT IS THE ROLE OF THE CHURCH IN THE COMING AGE OF INFORMATION?

Megatrends need megaTruth. The church of Jesus Christ is entrusted with the final and authoritative Word of God and we have been promised the continuing application of truth through the Spirit of God. Working together through the mind of the believer and the message of the church, the Word and the Spirit teach us, correct us and direct us as we face the trends of the times. Therefore, in the Age of Information when truth is up for grabs, the church is just coming into its own. Away with the pessimism that dubs our day "The Post-Christian Era." Whenever ultimate truth is at stake, the church contests on its own turf, chooses its own weapons and sets its own game plan. The apostle Paul sounds our battle cry for the Age of Information.

> For though we walk in the flesh, we do not war according to the flesh.
>
> For the weapons of our warfare are not carnal but mighty through God for
>
> pulling down strongholds,

casting down arguments and every high thing that
exalts itself against the knowledge of God,

bringing every thought into captivity to the obedience
of Christ (2 Corinthians 10:3-5,NKJV).

**MEGATRUTH IS THE CHRISTIAN RESPONSE
TO MEGATRENDS.**

PART I

CRISIS OF TRUTH

New information in the hands of the people creates a Crisis of Truth: in the society, either revolution or reformation; in the church, either apostasy or awakening.

19

2.
Reading the Signs of the Times

Yogi Berra, my favorite folk philosopher, spoke an inadvertent mouthful when he said, "You can observe a lot just by watching." His wisdom, however bumbling it may sound, matches the perceptive insight of one of the smartest persons I ever knew. Harold Pepinsky, a professor at Ohio State University and a household name in social psychology, appeared at the door of my faculty office one morning wearing an impish grin and a balloon-sized lapel pin. On the pin were emblazoned the big blue letters, "T.O.C.S." I instantly indulged the plea on his face by asking, "What does 'T.O.C.S.' mean?"

With childlike glee, the renowned Dr. Pepinsky finger-walked his way across the letters, announcing as he went, "Thoughtful Observer of the Contemporary Scene." With Yogi, he knew that you can "observe" a lot just by watching.

Jesus minced no words in responding to the Pharisees who demanded that He give them a sign from heaven to prove His authority.

> He sighed deeply in his spirit, and saith, "Why doth
> this generation seek after a sign? Verily I say unto

you, There shall no sign be given unto this generation" (Mark 8:12).

In Matthew's Gospel, Jesus answered the Pharisees' request
with a note of surprise:

> When it is evening, ye say, It will be fair weather:
> for the sky is red. And in the morning, It will be
> foul weather today: for the sky is red and lowering.
> O ye hypocrites, ye can discern the face of the sky;
> but can ye not discern the signs of the times?
> (Matthew 16:2,3).

Why does Jesus refuse to give them a sign, while expecting
them to read the signs in the sky? Because there is a difference
between disbelief and discernment. Disbelief demands a sign
which requires no faith and short-circuits the work of God. If
Jesus had given the Pharisees a sign, He would have joined
the ranks of the magicians, charlatans and hucksters who wan-
dered the countryside telling fortunes. Furthermore, Jesus knew
that signs from heaven must be continuously reinforced and
escalated in order to maintain belief based upon miracles.
Giving a sign would have been sin for Jesus; asking for a sign
revealed the sin of the Pharisees.

Discerning the signs of the times is an entirely different
matter. While refusing to give a sign from heaven, Jesus expected
the Pharisees to read the signs of the times as effectively as
they read the natural signs in the sky. History and prophecy
converged with current and relevant meaning when Jesus re-
ponded,

> There shall no sign be given . . . but the sign of
> the prophet Jonas (Matthew 12:39).

The message is clear. Jesus rejected signs from heaven as
a test of faith, yet He expects us to watch the trends as part
of our responsibility for spiritual discernment. *Megatrends* is a
report on the signs of the times. It is not gospel truth, but it

gives us signs to which we must respond as "thoughtful observers of the contemporary scene."

THE "SCIENCE" OF TREND-WATCHING

Our beginning point is to understand the way in which Naisbitt developed the ten megatrends. His basic assumption is that we can best predict the future by understanding the present. Newspapers, then, become the source of current information which can be projected on a trend line into the future. Over a period of years, Naisbitt's group has collected, counted and compiled newspaper articles from across the country. The subjects that receive the most frequent and continuing attention become the profile of the present upon which the future can be projected. By this 'technique of trend-watching, Naisbitt observed the ten new directions that he has labeled "megatrends."

However, there are weaknesses in Naisbitt's approach. Newspapers and other popular media can be slanted toward events that are superficial and momentary rather than foundational and lasting. In television newscasting, for instance, the rule of reporting is, "If it doesn't light up or blow up, don't report it." To compete with that kind of reporting, newspapers are inevitably pushed toward the sensational and saleable story. If so, the news media set trends as well as reflect them. The moral responsibility of the media for influencing the values of our society is not addressed by Naisbitt.

Still, his method of research deserves attention. As we need history to interpret the present, we need the present to predict the future. Otherwise, we are condemned to repeat the past, be unrealistic in the present and fantasize about the future. If, therefore, we recognize the weakness of Naisbitt's technique and remember that he suggests it as the "best," not the only, way to predict the future, his fundamental premise is sound enough to raise this question,

WHAT CAN WE LEARN ABOUT OUR SPIRITUAL FUTURE BY READING *MEGATRENDS?*

Each year, editors of the *Evangelical Newsletter* survey evangelical leaders and report on the spiritual trends they see for the coming year. The Christianity Today Institute, as well, has gone into evangelical trend-watching. This book will join several others that address the future of the church based upon current trends. What are some of these trends?

The growing influence of the charismatic movement at home and abroad;

the shifting center of power from the First- to the Third-World church;

the continuing breakdown of the family;

the growing accommodation of Christians to the values of self-interest, secularism and materialism;

the increasing interest in spiritual formation;

the rise of evangelism in the mainline denominations;

the changing emphasis upon the pastoral role as an equipping ministry;

the growing emphasis on lay participation in ministry;

the spreading political activism of conservative Christians;

the continuing interest in relational theology and the building of community;

the growing "consumer" mentality applied to religious choices;

the increasing tension among Christians over such
issues as economics, nuclear arms, and pro-life questions.

This list is neither complete nor final. A quick review shows
that these trends are subject to rising and falling action. Yet,
beneath the ebb and flow of waves on the surface, there is a
tide which will determine the direction of evangelical Christianity
for years to come. We share Naisbitt's observation that we can
best predict our future by understanding our present — spiritually
as well as socially.

While pursuing his task of trend-watching, Naisbitt developed three other premises upon which *Megatrends* is built.
First, he noted that most of the ten trends began in one of
five flagship states — California, Florida, Washington, Colorado
or Connecticut.[1] This observation requires a megashift in our
thinking. New York City and Washington, D.C., are presumed
to be the places where trends are set. Not so, according to
Naisbitt. The leadership of the nation is moving south and west
away from New York City and toward the Hi/Tech world of
the information industry. New York City is holding on to its
image as the financial capital of the nation, but many people
fail to realize that the new wealth is information, not money.
Likewise, the center of power has shifted from Washington,
D.C., to state and local governments, even though Capitol Hill
retains its reputation as the power hub of the nation. Naisbitt
says that, at present, California is the leader of the flagship
states but that Florida may take over that position.

ARE THE FLAGSHIPS FOR SPIRITUAL TRENDS
SHIFTING AS WELL?

New York City has never been a power base for evangelical
Christianity. On the contrary, the Big Apple is best described
as an "evangelical wasteland." The shift of power away from
New York City will make little difference in spiritual trends.
However, it should remind us of our tendency to bypass tough
places at home while on our way out to evangelize the world.

Washington, D.C., has become just the opposite for us. In recent years, there has been an evangelical stampede toward the capital city. Presumably, national identity for Christian denominations and organizations is not complete until a Washington office has been established. There is no doubt but that an "evangelical Christian presence" in the Capitol has been helpful in monitoring regulations, lobbying for legislation, and testifying on legal issues which affect the church and its mission. While much of the effort has been given to preserving the rights of the church, the public perception is that the movement is seeking political power to both protect church privileges and impose its beliefs upon the nation. The dilemma of a negative public image is secondary, however, to the question, Is the center of power shifting from Washington, D.C., to state and local governments? If it is, we evangelicals have demonstrated once again our unique ability to awaken late, rush pell-mell in the wrong direction, and arrive at our destination just after the meeting has been adjourned.

Look at the question another way. How many of the current trends in the church started in Washington, D.C., or in such traditional places of evangelical influence as Wheaton, Illinois; Wilmore, Kentucky; Nashville, Tennessee; or Dallas, Texas?

The answer is not immediately obvious. We need Naisbitt's second observation supporting his basic premise to help us out. He writes that trends move from the bottom up, but fads start at the top and move down.[2] *Does this premise apply to spiritual as well as social trends?* When we think about the origin and direction of such trends as the charismatic influence, family issues, spiritual formation, mainline evangelism, lay participation, political activism and the need for community, we realize that they did not begin in traditional places of religious power. Nor are they moving from the top down. They originated at the grassroots in places not unlike California, Florida, Washington, Colorado and Connecticut, and are moving from bottom up to challenge religious hierarchies and their leadership.

Returning once again to the list of trends, we gain another insight. Missing are: inerrancy as an issue, church growth as a movement, and ecumenical organization as a goal. Are these examples of "top down" issues initiated by leaders in traditional places? Do they flash like fads for a moment of time without the sustaining power at the grassroots level to form a trend upon which the future can be predicted? If so, trend-watchers will want to follow with a critical eye other issues, like the rising power of the papacy in the Roman Catholic Church, the role of women in ministry, the persistent efforts toward unity among mainline Protestant denominations, the protest against nuclear arms, the economics of hunger and poverty, the increased use of liturgy in worship, and the extension of political activism toward a Christian lobby. Each issue can be tested by the questions, What's the place of its origin? and, Is it moving from top down or bottom up?

Of course, the trends that will revolutionize the church are those that release a synergetic power by bringing the grassroots and the hierachy together in a two-way movement between the bottom and the top. Among the current trends, abortion is the issue that comes closest to being a revolutionary force in our century. As pro-life leaders try to extend the issue to protest contraception or passive euthanasia for hopelessly terminal cases, however, they may weaken the case by shifting the power away from the grassroots and changing the direction of influence from bottom up to top down. Therefore, as a working premise, we can say

SPIRITUAL MEGATRENDS
WHICH WILL TRANSFORM THE CHURCH
MOVE FROM THE BOTTOM UP.

The third supporting premise that Naisbitt follows in his study of trends is that *a society can deal with only one issue at a time.*[3] The principle applies equally to individuals and institutions. If we are bombarded with issues, we must sort them out by priority and deal with them in sequence one at a time. The layout of newspapers illustrates this premise. The top right-hand corner of the front page is the place for the headline story because people look there first. Thus, there are never two headlines in a good newspaper. Someone has to make a decision. A secondary headline most often will be placed in the top right-hand corner of the third page, because that is where readers naturally look when they open the newspaper.

Confusion reigns in a society or an institution when issues are not sorted out and acted upon one at a time. Especially in a "time of parenthesis," Naisbitt says that the most important question is, What business are we in? For our society, he would say that our current business is to recognize that we are rapidly passing from the Age of Industry to the Age of Information. In this time of transition, however, the limits of our social energy require that we deal with one issue at a time. Naisbitt calls this process making "forced choices in a closed system." In other words, our system for assimilating information can handle only so many issues. When the system fills up, we close it off against the entry of any new issues, and we are forced to choose one with which we will deal.

Forced choices must also be made when our system of religious issues fills up. In the past decade, we can trace in sequence the national issues — abortion, family, feminism, nuclear arms, pornography — which have marched at the head of our public witness. Within the evangelical Christian community, there has been another parade of in-house issues. Charismatic renewal, inerrancy, church growth, women in ministry, lay participation, the electronic church, fundamentalism, evangelical leadership and heresy tests all have been a part of the passing parade. Evidently, we try to handle one external and one internal issue at a time. Externally, evangelicals are still identified with issues of *personal morality* which the secular public considers private matters; internally, issues of *theological orthodoxy* dominate the evangelical debate. The rule of thumb seems to be: If the subculture is threatened from without, public morality is wrong; if the subculture is threatened from within, personal theology is wrong. Assuming that our current responses to external and internal changes constitute a megatrend which will persist in the future, we can predict:

EVANGELICAL CHRISTIANS WILL CONTINUE
TO BE IDENTIFIED WITH SOCIAL ISSUES
OF PERSONAL MORALITY AND RELIGIOUS ISSUES
OF THEOLOGICAL ORTHODOXY.

What's missing in *Megatrends*? Even though James Naisbitt is currently the leading guru for the future, *Megatrends* is not gospel truth. As we have already noted, Naisbitt is an advocate of the New Age movement which is reputed to be a revelation of redemption that is superior to Christianity. Therefore, in reading and relating its findings to our spiritual future, Christians must fervently seek the mind of the discerning Spirit of God.

If evangelical Christians have a fault line in reading the signs of the times, it is the tendency to make panaceas out of partial truth. When *I'm O.K., You're O.K.* came out in the 1960s, evangelical Christians joined the rush to buy the book. To many, it became a companion with the Bible in small group discussions. More recently, M. Scott Peck's best-seller, *The Road Less Traveled,* has become an evangelical favorite. Few persons, however, stop to ask questions about the fundamental propositions which guide the authors of these books. Without critical thinking and spiritual discernment, we will succumb to the idolatry of best-sellers. Do not misunderstand the point. Each of the books has something valuable for Christians, but only as the discerning mind of the Spirit helps us sort out the truth in relationship to the Word of God. Therefore, we must reemphasize:

CHRISTIANS MUST HAVE THE SPIRIT OF GOD
TO READ THE SIGNS OF THE TIMES AND DISCERN
THE SPIRITUAL TRUTH OF *MEGATRENDS*.

Long-range or strategic planning is a co-partner with trend-watching. In *Megatrends,* Naisbitt sounds so certain and so final in his predictions. The truth of the matter is that the scoring percentage on his predictions is not too much better than The Great Criswell or Jeane Dixon. He predicted, for

instance, that Jimmy Carter would win the 1980 presidential
election. To cover his flank, Naisbitt publishes a quarterly *Trend
Report*. Through this newsletter, one of his megatrends has
already been revised. Naisbitt predicted the growing movement
of corporations and people from the industrial North to the
Hi/Tech South and West. Now, however, he finds that cities in
the Northeast and North Central regions have taken it upon
themselves to create an economic and cultural environment
which is causing Hi/Tech corporations to rethink their location.
The revision of the megatrend reminds me of the advice given
by a friend who served under President Truman with the responsibility for long-term economic planning, "If you must plan,
plan often." The same type of advice could be applied to
reading *Megatrends:*

IF YOU MUST PREDICT, PREDICT OFTEN.

Something more profound is missing from *Megatrends*.
Naisbitt's predictions are made on a straight line moving upward.
Human history is never so neat. The straight line may turn out
to be a circle and the rising line may fall. Herman Kahn, who
might be called the father of futurists, recognized the fallacy
of predictions based upon a straight line rising upward.[4] While
acknowledging the value of projecting current trends into the
future, he also made provision for jumps along the trend line
and surprises which sent the line off in another direction. The
invention of the laser beam in the early 1970s is an example.
According to the straight line projection, the laser beam would
not become a functional instrument until the 1980s. Suddenly,
however, laser research made breakthroughs that brought the
instrument into being ten years ahead of its time! Kahn called
this jump along the trend line a "serendipity," which he expects
to be repeated time and time again in the future. Whenever
scientific research or social forces merge into a critical mass,
a new invention or movement erupts as a breakthrough.

Even with the recognition that trend lines are not always
straight and rising, Kahn missed one of the most significant
surprises of the 1970s. His predictions in the book, *The Year*

2000, which was published in 1968, failed to foresee the "Born-again" movement of the mid-1970s. For Christians, this is good news. No one can predict the surprises that the Spirit of God has in store for us. Whether resurrection, reformation or revival, God has an impish twinkle in His eye. He may move along the line of current trends, but when He comes, it is always with an element of surprise. Therefore, while we must take megatrends seriously, we hold them lightly.

GOD HAS A FUTURE FILLED WITH SURPRISES.

Megatrends is also a description of movement on the surface of our society. Even though Naisbitt says that the trends will transform our lives, he pays little attention to the underlying moral tensions which are interlaced with social change. Yankelovich, in his popular but less celebrated book, *New Rules: Living in a World Turned Upside Down,* deals directly with the underground stirrings in moral values which may erupt in the future to change radically our social landscape.[5] Particularly in moral values related to sex, marriage, and family, Yankelovich finds a megashift of attitude in the past twenty-five years. Premarital sex is an example. In 1958, 80 percent of the general public condemned sex before marriage; in 1978, 80 percent accepted it without condemnation. Although the shift may not be quite so dramatic, similar swings can be detected in attitudes toward divorce, cohabitation, extra-marital sex and homosexuality. Yankelovich feels that we may be lulled to sleep by a conservative swing toward traditional values on the surface of our society. He detects the sound of absolute and relative moral values rumbling "underground" against each other like the action of subterranean plates before an earthquake. Yankelovich sees some hope for relief from the tension in people seeking a sense of community and commitment when they find that radical self-interest is a dead end. Nevertheless, the moral tension continues to mount and an eruption appears to be inevitable.

Christians must be able to read the signs on the earth as well as in the sky. In fact, moral megashifts may be more pronounced in our future than social megatrends. Naisbitt seems to separate the two. He leaves the moral and spiritual implications of his megatrends for others to work out. This is our task.

MORAL MEGASHIFTS ARE AT LEAST AS IMPORTANT TO OUR SPIRITUAL FUTURE AS SOCIAL MEGATRENDS.

No miraculuous sign from heaven is needed to know the direction in which the world is moving. The signs in our society which lead us to predict our future are as obvious as the natural signs in the sky which lead us to predict the weather. To ignore those societal signs is to become like dinosaurs waiting for the weather to change or like dodo birds waiting to sprout wings. But to be dictated to by those signs is to become like a dead fish washed along with the tide. The danger is false optimism or fatal pessimism. Jesus notes that the only sign from heaven for a wicked and adulterous generation is the sign of the prophet Jonah whose life epitomized the sinful rebellion of man and the gracious redemption of God. Spiritual discernment is essential for keeping the biblical balance between optimism and pessimism in reading the signs of the times.

CHRISTIANS ARE OPTIMISTIC ABOUT OUR HUMAN FUTURE BECAUSE WE ARE REALISTIC ABOUT SIN IN HUMAN NATURE AND ASSURED OF GRACE IN GOD'S NATURE.

Utterly dependent upon the discerning Spirit, then, we can

interpret the spiritual meaning of *Megatrends;*

choose our options for a more effective Christian witness in the coming Age of Information; and

anticipate being alive as Christians in a "time of parenthesis" between eras of human civilization.

THE STAGE IS SET
FOR A GREAT SPIRITUAL AWAKENING!

3.
Living in a Time of Parenthesis

Christians are people suspended in paradox. Only faith can understand the paradox of truth when Jesus says

> to lose is to gain;
> to lead is to serve;
> to live is to die.

As perplexing as the paradox of truth may be, we can handle it better than the paradox of time. Again, Jesus poses our problem when, in Luke 19:13, He commands the stewards among whom He distributed the talents:

Occupy till I come.

Present and future time are critically balanced in this command. The temptation is to become preoccupied with either the present or the future. Secularism is essentially a time orientation to the present. Its extreme expression is to squeeze time into the "radical now" and neglect both the past and the future.

"Yuppies" (young, urban professionals) who were interviewed
for the *Wall Street Journal* showed their secular time orientation
when they admitted little interest in retirement plans because
of their uncertainty about the future. "Buy Now and Worry
Later" or "Play Now and Pay Later" is their motto.

Periodically, Christians go to the other extreme. We are
often preoccupied with the future and focused upon the second
coming of Christ. Most often, this tendency to fix upon the
end-time to the neglect of the present rises out of social despair,
economic disadvantage or religious persecution. In the context
of the "national malaise" that gripped the United States in the
1970s after Watergate, we should not be surprised that *The
Late Great Planet Earth* topped all best-selling lists for the
decade. If the book is an indicator of the social and spiritual
climate of the times, our despair ran deeper and wider than
we might have thought. Perhaps the columnist was right who
said, "Our circle of sanity was badly bent and almost broken."

Naisbitt falls into a different time trap in *Megatrends.* As
a disciple of the New Age Movement, he plays down the
transitional present in favor of the transformational future.
Again, it is not by accident that he chooses the subtitle for his
book "Ten Trends *Transforming* Our Lives" (italics mine). Consistent with the New Age philosophy, he sees the present being
pulled onward and upward into the future on the rising consciousness of the transcendent mind. His final shout, "My God, what
a fantastic time to be alive!" is more theological than scientific.
Naisbitt is an optimistic humanist of the first order.

TO LIVE AS A CHRISTIAN
IN A TIME OF PARENTHESIS
IS TO LIVE AS A REALISTIC OPTIMIST.

We cannot deny the fact that we are in a time of cataclysmic
change that is affecting the whole of our lives. We cannot
ignore the evidence of speeding trends that are propelling us
forward into the Age of Information. If we respond to Jesus'
command, "Occupy til I come," we must use the knowledge

of our changing times as wisely as Jesus expected the stewards to invest their money. Naisbitt reminds us that information, not money, is the new wealth and the new capital of the coming age. Therefore, we must assume that the principle of stewardship holds for information as much as for money. Entrepreneurs always flourish in a time of transition. So why not think of ourselves as stewards of information which God has entrusted to us for investment in risk-taking ventures that will multiply the effectiveness of the gospel and glorify His name?

TO LIVE AS A CHRISTIAN
IN A TIME OF PARENTHESIS
IS TO LIVE AS A STEWARD OF TRUST.

Jesus challenges us to be meaningfully engaged in the present while anticipating the future moment when He will come again. In its root meaning, the word "occupy" is a business term which connotes the responsibility of making a wise investment with the view to a multiple return. The steward of God must never fall victim to the idolatry of the present. As a check-and-balance, everything we do must be done with the knowledge that we will give an accounting for our stewardship when our Lord returns. Our fathers put the biblical time perspective into a capsule when they wrote the creed, "The chief end of man is to glorify God."

TO LIVE AS A CHRISTIAN
IN A TIME OF PARENTHESIS
IS TO LIVE WITH TRAUMA.

Civilization never changes easily. When Naisbitt advances the thesis that we are living in a time of parenthesis between eras of human civilization, he is predicting trauma at the heart of our society. If he is right, three areas will show the wounds of change. First, *traditional values* will no longer provide the moral pathways for coping with change. Second, *established institutions,* especially the home, church and school, will be shaken at their foundations. Third, *legitimate leaders* will suffer the loss of public confidence, not only in their ability to guide the society toward its goals, but in their personal integrity as well.

Anyone who lived through the stormy 1960s and the serious 1970s will have no doubt that we are living in a time of parenthesis. A sexual revolution took place that tried to turn traditional moral pathways into trails trod by an outmoded minority. Or perhaps a more fitting description would be that once-hidden footpaths for pre-marital affairs, cohabitation and homosexuality became public thoroughfares. The moral impact of the sexual revolution, indelibly imprinted on our national character, is symptomatic of a more fundamental change in the foundations of our society. Behind the sexual revolution is the quintessential moral question, Are moral values absolute or relative? Your source of authority determines your answer. According to the Word of God, human sexuality is sacred and the standard for human sexual behavior is absolute. To strip sex of its sanctity and base our standards of sexual behavior on situation ethics is to create anarchy in morality. Even secular observers are quick to note that the moral consensus undergirding our society has been eroded. Put succinctly, "The moral throne is empty."

SELF-INTEREST IS THE PRETENDER
WHO HAS MOUNTED THE MORAL THRONE.

Coincidental with the "Born-again" movement in the middle 1970s, the "Me" generation came to life among us. While the "Born-again" movement gained public attention with its numbers, the "Me" generation converted our private attitudes.

Christopher Lasch, in his perceptive book, *The Culture of Narcissism,* identifies the creed of the cult as belief in the "Radical Now," the "Radical Self," and the "Radical Right to Happiness."[1] To portray the character which is created by this creed, Lasch chooses Narcissus, the boy-god of Greek mythology. When Narcissus sees his own face in the mirror of a reflecting pool, he instantly falls in love with his own image. Like the flower, he bends over the pool, doting on his own reflection. Totally absorbed in this self-love, Narcissus finally withers away from the frustration of being unable to consummate his desire.

Failing to learn the lesson of Narcissus, Robert Ringer translates the cult of self-interest into a working rule of life in his best-selling book, *Looking Out for Number One.*[2] His code of behavior is simple: *Weigh every human transaction on the scales of self-interest.* If the balance tips to your own personal happiness, do it. If not, negotiate and manipulate until the weight is in your favor.

Whether we realize it or not, the erosion of our established institutions — the home, church and school — is a direct result of rampant self-interest. In the late 1960s and 1970s, every identifiable "institution" came under fire. Not by accident, our schools took the brunt of a frontal attack against traditional authority. More subtly, but with even greater devastation, the foundations of the home as a social institution began to crumble. If current trends continue, by 1990 the majority of children will come from single-parent homes. The ripple effect will be felt throughout every segment of our society, from the economic discrepancy between "haves" and "have-nots" to the spiritual deprivation of people whose needs are not met by the traditional ministries of the church.

Single-parent families need compassion, not condemnation. They are only symptomatic of the desacrilization of marriage and the drive toward self-interest. Social institutions, such as the home, must be held together by a commitment in which self-interest is sacrificed for the common good. Without this commitment, institutions lose their purpose and power. Amitai Etzioni, a sociologist at George Washington University, believes that we are witnessing the "hollowing of America" as the radical self-interest of the "Me" generation of the 1970s is impacting our established institutions in the 1980s.[3]

Like dominoes in a row, when traditional moral values fall and established institutions topple, confidence in legitimate leadership is soon to follow. Authority that is inherent in position becomes suspect. Leadership decisions are called into question,

not so much on substance as on process. Unless everyone
participates in a decision, no ownership is claimed and no
responsibility is accepted. So, the leader must earn the right
to lead in every new decision. Even then, there is no equity
of trust which carries over from one decision to another. Broken
trust in human relationships is both the cause and effect of the
loss of confidence in legitimate leadership.

IN A TIME OF PARENTHESIS, AUTHORITY BREAKS DOWN AND SELF-INTEREST RISES.

The dominance of self-interest and the breakdown of authority, then, are the primary symptoms of the trauma of living in
a time of parenthesis. Naisbitt does not deal with these issues
as megatrends. Of course, he hints at the idea that thinking
machines threaten self-worth and networks of information appeal
to self-interest, but he does not explore these trends in a moral
and spiritual context. In fact, he is criticized by friend and foe
alike for failing to mention the plight of the poor and the
elderly who, in multiplying numbers, will be social casualties
in the Age of Information. Consistent with the New Age promise
of rising human consciousness, he ignores the social and spiritual
fallout which requires new depths of compassion for the victims
of high technology. Naisbitt exposes his defective view of
human nature and his deficient response to human need. His
straight lines rise into Utopia. Intoxicated by unbridled optimism,
Naisbitt fails to realize the need for spiritual renewal in the
transformation of our society.

IN A TIME OF PARENTHESIS, SOCIAL TRANSFORMATION DEPENDS UPON SPIRITUAL RENEWAL.

While one era of history cannot be imposed upon another,
we can learn from the pattern of the past. England in the
eighteenth century went through a time of parenthesis between
the dying Age of Agriculture and the dawning Age of Industry.

Technology led the way with the invention of the steam engine. Every component of English culture shuddered from the shock of change. As people moved from stable village communities to urban ghettos, traditional moral values were left behind and moral corruption became the mode of human behavior. Established institutions were devastated. The home, in particular, broke down. The established church, caught in the comfort of its rural stature and village authority, failed to move with the masses or meet their changing needs. Schools of the eighteenth century, as well, held on to their elitist expectations and classical studies. So, with its established institutions either broken down or stuck in place, English society lost its moorings and floundered in a sea of cultural chaos.

To show the extent of the social trauma in eighteenth-century England, even the long-established legitimate leadership of the English monarchy suffered irreparable loss. The divine right of kings had already been broken by the *Magna Charta* in A.D. 1215. In the eighteenth century, an act of Parliament shifted the governing authority from the monarchy to the people through representative government. Overnight, the king became a "paper prince," with only the power of protocol. In its "time of parenthesis," England teetered on the edge of anarchy, and like its neighbor France, became ripe for revolution.

Scholars of eighteenth-century history do not hesitate to credit the Wesleyan Revival for saving England from the bloody revolt which forced France to its knees. Under the leadership of the Spirit of God, John and Charles Wesley went into the industrial ghetto, preached free salvation for all in the open market, sang songs of love divine in the melodies of the day, and provided alternative structures for the broken home, the stagnant church and the elitist school. Out of personal revival came social reform. Humanitarian laws were enacted against slavery, child labor, brutalization of prisoners and exploitation of the poor. Thus, England came through its "time of parenthesis" without a violent revolution and entered the Age of Industry with a climate of justice and compassion for the needs of its people.

AMERICAN HISTORY GIVES US A PATTERN
FOR SPIRITUAL REVIVAL AND SOCIAL REFORM.

Students of the great awakenings in American history find
a pattern leading from spiritual revival to social reform. In his
book, *Revivals, Awakening and Reform,* McLoughlin suggests
a loosely connected, five-stage model for a great spiritual
awakening.[4]

Stage I is characterized by *individual stress.* Awakenings
always begin in troubled times. When moral consensus breaks
down under the weight of social change, individuals are the
first to feel the stress. Uncertainties about life, sex, marriage,
and human relationships create what sociologists call "anomie"
— free-floating anxiety in the absence of a moral center.

Stage II follows with *cultural disjuncture.* Sooner or later,
the breakdown of what Andrew Greeley calls "plausible social
supports" rumbles through established institutions of the society.
Colleges and universities are usually the first to feel the vented
stress of the young, but soon the impact ripples out to the
home, the church, the business community and the government.
Leaders of these institutions always become the focus for
frustration as they suffer the loss of credibility.

Recovery begins with Stage III — a period of *spiritual
revival.* Before revival, however, a conservative swing can be
detected in the culture as people try to rescue lost values and
restore crumbling institutions. Nativists call for a return to
manifest destiny, fundamentalists search for Scriptures to justify
a national religion, and public opinion clamors for scapegoats
who can be sent off into the wilderness with the sins of the
nation upon their heads.

A revival does not settle a culture, it disturbs it. Like the
penetrating point of a high-pressure system which creates a
tornado-like turbulence in a mass of heavy air, a great awakening
is in the making, but it is not guaranteed. More often than
not, revivalistic movements have died when what Martin Marty
calls the "bubble and fizz" are gone.

Stage IV of a great awakening is the time for *prophetic voices*. Great awakenings in the past have had stand-out evangelists, such as Edwards, Whitefield, Finney and Moody, but they have not been identified with a single person. Instead, many prophetic voices have been raised to beckon born-again people to follow them through the moral mazeway toward Christian behavior in a changed social setting. These prophets are not wild-eyed seers; they are conservatives who call the people back to biblical standards of social justice and demand that they be applied once again in the contemporary scene. By definition, their ministry is usually brief and unpopular because they call both the church and the culture to repentance. Without prophets, there can be no reformers.

Stage V is the time for *social renewal and reform*. Following the prophets, reformers can now come forward with a vision of hope for cultural renewal. Reformers always speak the good word of hope for the needs of a new generation. Built upon unchanging biblical values, the terms of God's covenant provide guidelines for restoring viability to social institutions and credibility for institutional leadership.

In the Great Awakening of eighteenth-century America, those who recognized God's covenant for that generation were named "New Lights." Not unexpectedly, the "New Lights" shone first among young people on Christian college campuses. In great spiritual awakenings, students break early from the old order, respond to the prophets' call for renewal, and lead the way into positions of influence in society. Through those positions they influence social reform based upon the moral principles of God's covenant, applying them to their generation.

REVIVALS NEVER QUALIFY AS GREAT AWAKENINGS
UNTIL THE CULTURE SHOWS SIGNS
OF MORAL RENEWAL AND SOCIAL REFORM.

Using this five-stage model as a guide, we ask the question, In our "time of parenthesis," are we in the midst of a great awakening?

Individual stress, the symptom of Stage I, began about 1960 when cracks appeared in our confidence in American superiority. John F. Kennedy's assassination split us wide open. As noted at that time, the circle of our sanity almost broke. Stress drove individuals toward encounter groups, psychological counselors, cults, self-awareness books, the "Jesus movement," motivational workshops and ecstatic religious experiences. As always, the tension surfaced in self-doubts about life, death, sex, marriage, family and other human relationships. Evangelical Christianity responded to these fissures in our confidence with a relational theology and its manifold expressions of spiritual therapy. In fact, if a list were made of evangelical Christianity's contributions to our culture since the stress-filled '60s, relational literature would have to be at the top. More than marketing is involved when you see such books as Robert Schuller's *The Be-Happy Attitudes* and Charles Swindoll's *Growing Seasons* featured among best-sellers in secular bookstores, or M. Scott Peck's *The Road Less Traveled* near the top of the list of books that students on college and university campuses are reading. Whether our literature is feeding self-interest, relieving guilt, or creating a desire for spiritual conversion is unknown. We can give the benefit of the doubt to our relational literature having a positive spiritual impact upon the secular culture because the Holy Spirit so often creates good out of that which we criticize.

Stage II — cultural disjuncture — came upon us in the mid-1960s when traditional institutions came under attack. Universities were the first victims of the wrath of the young at Berkeley and Columbia. Corporations, government, and financial institutions followed. Of course, at the center of the storm were the leaders of those insititutions, who still have not recovered their loss of credibility. In the aftershock of these ruptures, the home and the church were also damaged. Particularly among the young, the church was perceived as another waning institution under leaders of questionable credibility. The young are not alone. When confidence in traditional institutions declines, new associations arise. In our generation, parachurch ministries have sprung up like dandelions on a summer lawn.

Although their leaders might deny the point, parachurch ministries arise as signs of cultural disjunctures; they are judgments, however polite, that the established church is ineffective in the critical role of responding to changing human needs.

The prelude for Stage III — spiritual revival — was the resignation of Richard Nixon in 1974. A nativistic swing to the right was already under way and, even though Nixon identified himself with that movement, the pendulum did not stop with his betrayal of national trust. Public opinion reacted with another push of the pendulum toward capitalism, conservatism and cultural Christianity. Nixon himself became the scapegoat, sent into the wilderness of San Clemente with the sins of the nation upon his head.

These events set the stage for the revival of the 1970s. Gallup announced the "Born-again" movement with a poll showing that 45 million Americans (33 percent of the nation) professed to be "Bible-believing, born-again, witnessing Christians." Later, he proclaimed 1976 as The Year of the Evangelical and had his crystal ball polished when Jimmy Carter was elected President.

Deeper analysis of the "Born-again" movement shows it centered in the South, led by charismatics, and disseminated through electronic media. Video religion moved the masses. Although panned as regional, anti-intellectual and hucksterish, the new brand of evangelicalism relieved individual stress and restored a form of institutional support. Twentieth-century television therapy replaced eighteenth-century tombstone preaching as the revivalistic means of reaching the masses.

Stage IV — the time for prophetic voices is upon us. In the 1980s, the destiny of spiritual awakening in our generation will be settled. Either prophets will rise to call for biblical justice and repentance for the church, or the "Born-again" movement will disappear in "bubble and fizz."

One does not have to be a prophet to know where biblical justice and repentance are needed. Evangelical Christianity must be extricated from the secular mire that is sucking the life out of the church. Christian behavior needs redefining; Christian

institutions need reshaping. Christian leadership needs renewal
and Christian ethics need reworking. Again, because we are
too close to the situation to be objective, it may take the
perspective of time to hear the echo of prophetic voices that
are speaking today. Charles Colson may well be remembered
as a prophetic voice, raised up of God and anointed by the
Holy Spirit, calling for social justice in the society and spiritual
renewal in the church. Standing on the bridge between the
church and society, he speaks and both worlds listen.

Stage V — social renewal — is still farther into the future.
Sometime in the 1980s, we will know whether or not the
prophetic voices have spoken and have been heard. If so, we
can anticipate New Lights for the twentieth century seeing
God's covenant for our generation.

At present, we must be skeptical about the efforts at social
reform rising out of evangelical Christianity. In most instances,
the connection between social justice and societal reform is
weak. Our crusades are centered upon abortion, pornography,
media decency, religious freedom in public schools, substance
abuse, and protection of the family. By and large, these issues
are cast in relation to personal morality rather than social justice.
If historical patterns hold, a great awakening depends upon the
"Born-again" movement maturing into a spiritual cause for
social justice in our century. We await individual Christian
leaders who penetrate the institutional centers of power with
the natural movement of their skills and the conscious motive
of their witness. It has happened before; it can happen again.
If God wills, born-again and Spirit-filled Christians will have
the opportunity to lead the way into another Great Spiritual
Awakening in American history. As of today, the jury is still out.

How will we come through our "time of parenthesis" into
the Age of Information? The alternatives for the church are:
awakening, or apostasy. We can fight aggressively, ignore bliss-
fully, or submit passively to the megatrends that are moving
through our society. If we do any of these, we will default on
our responsibility to influence the direction of change.

**OUR GOAL MUST BE TO EMERGE
FROM OUR TIME OF PARENTHESIS
INTO THE AGE OF INFORMATION
WITH THE SPIRITUAL STRENGTH OF A RENEWED
PEOPLE,
A REVIVED CHURCH,
AND A REFORMED SOCIETY.**

4.
Anticipating the Age of Information

We are coming through our "time of parenthesis." And on the other side, we are entering the Age of Information. In that Age, every component of our culture and every aspect of our lives will be influenced by new, changing and multiplying information sources and systems. *Megatrends* is essentially a look at information as a strategic resource which can make us masters or slaves of high technology. Information can make us more

> human or inhuman;
> moral or immoral;
> wise or unwise.

INFORMATION CAN ALSO MAKE US MORE SPIRITUAL OR UNSPIRITUAL.

In a very practical sense, Jesus introduced a new age of information in His day. Scribes, Pharisees and Sadduccees had exclusive hold on information related to the kingdom of God until He came. His preaching and teaching broke the stranglehold of the religious establishment when He took His message directly to the masses. Consistent with the pattern for a spiritual awakening, the message of Jesus promised new life for the people, broke through the stodgy tradition of the religious establishment, and disputed the moral authority of the religious leadership. Yet He did not leave the people without an affirmative message. In one of His first public statements, He declared,

> The Spirit of the Lord is upon me, because he hath anointed me to preach the gospel to the poor; he hath sent me to heal the brokenhearted, to preach deliverance to the captives, and recovering of sight to the blind, to set at liberty them that are bruised, to preach the acceptable year of the Lord (Luke 4:18,19).

History gives us another example. In the sixteenth century, Gutenberg invented the movable type printing press. No longer was it necessary for scribes to copy the texts by hand. With page after page rolling off the press, information multiplied and books became available for the masses. Of course, the Scriptures were the first to be printed. Almost overnight, the Roman Catholic Church, the Pope and the priests lost the power of privileged information. We know the result. Martin Luther led the way in disputing the tradition of the Church as the sole means of salvation, the decrees of the Pope as absolute authority, and the role of the priests as the exclusive intercessors between God and the people. Instead, the free grace of Jesus Christ became the sole means for salvation; the Scriptures became the sole authority for belief and practice; and personal communication with God in prayer became the means for intercession. The Reformation was a revolution of information.

Think forward into the coming Age of Information. When the mass of information available to the people again takes a quantum leap, can we predict another spiritual reformation? If so, what traditions of the church will be disputed? What moral authority will be tested? What leadership practices will fail?

No definitive answers can be given. We can, however, trace the current trends forward and see the spiritual challenge of expanding truth.

WHAT ARE THE MORAL AND SPIRITUAL IMPLICATIONS OF A NEW REVOLUTION OF INFORMATION?

Information is ENERGY. A few years ago, we were introduced to the concept called "entropy." It means that the physical resources of oil, gas, coal and uranium which have fueled the industrial society are exhaustible, and supplies are depleted as we use them. Without having solved this problem, we are now being introduced to the idea that information is also a resource, but one that is not depleted with use. In fact, information is a resource subject to the principle of "syntropy," not entropy. Syntropy is the principle of inexhaustible and self-generating resources which are intellectual or spiritual in nature. Love, for instance, is a spiritual resource that expands upon use. Information is the same way; it accumulates and multiplies. More than that, as new information converges with other new information, it produces a synergetic effect which expands the available information at an exponential rate. Information, then, does not accumulate on a straight line in multiplying jumps. Rather, it rises along a "J-curve" that begins at one level and then spurts upward on a line that is almost vertical.

Our problem for the future is unique in human history. We are being subjected to "information overload" as we are being bombarded with more facts, ideas, values and opinions than we can assimilate or interpret. A headline in the *New York Times* tells the story:

LIBRARIES ARE DROWNING IN A SEA OF INFORMATION

Our library systems are being swamped by an annual production of 800,000 books, 400,000 periodicals and untold thousands of documents in multiple copies. Who would have thought the time would come when the librarian of Yale University would throw up his hands and say, "We have too many books"? To voice his dilemma, he quotes from *Megatrends:* "We are drowning in information but starving for knowledge."[1]

At the National Association of Evangelicals convention a few years ago, President Reagan denounced Communist Russia as an "evil empire." Then he asked evangelicals to support the buildup of nuclear arms in his pending military budget. After the speech, one woman — who heard the Democrats' rebuttal and listened to the commentators' analyses — joined a debate in the lobby with the confession, "I don't know what to think."

We must not become victims of information overload. We must ask, How do we organize this information to make it meaningful? Our teaching/learning task is called *synthesizing.*

Information is VALUE. Another term needs to be added to our Hi/Tech vocabulary. "Information float" is the time it takes for a message to be transmitted from the sender to the receiver. Just 100 years ago, our communication systems required days for information to float across the country and weeks to float around the world. Naisbitt tells the story. When Abraham Lincoln was shot it took five days for the news to reach London. With the float time now reduced to milliseconds, London knew about the shooting of Ronald Reagan almost instantly. In fact, a reporter from the London newspaper *Spectator,* sitting at his typewriter one block away from the shooting, first heard the news when his London office called to send him to the scene.

The collapse of information float time has a direct bearing on the moral decisions that high technology demands of us. In the past we have had the luxury of time to process information before we have made a response. But high technology operates on breakthroughs, which result from accumulated information that converges into new knowledge with profound moral implications. Accumulation of information about the genetic structure of living organisms is the daring and dangerous frontier of high technology. Even now, new information about the genes and chromosomes is converging toward a breakthrough that will result in "gene machines." Their invention will bring into question our current ethical responses to the issues of life. We must ask the question, What is the standard by which we discern right and wrong, good and evil, in moral decisions? Our teaching/learning task of forming standards based on biblical principles is called *norming.*

Information is POWER. And who will control the flow of new information in the coming age? We know that whoever controls information controls the culture. In Orwell's *Nineteen Eighty-Four,* the central agency of government was the Ministry of Truth. By the manipulation of information, people were controlled without the use of force. With this in mind, let me introduce one more word for our Hi/Tech vocabulary. "Information pollution" is the danger that our communications systems will be controlled by the secular mind, or even manipulated by evil forces.

At the present time, the movie channels of cable television are economically sustained by the soft-core pornography of *R*-rated movies. Furthermore, cultic religious groups are buying into the communications industry in anticipation of controlling ideas and evangelizing the world. In studies sponsored by the Rockefeller Foundation, the conclusion is that the fields of communication, economics and public affairs will control the quality of our life in the future. Sad to say, these fields tend to be wastelands for evangelical Christians. With the dawning of the Age of Information, we must ask, Who will control our information sources and systems? This teaching/learning task is called *futuring,* or preparing for the challenges of the times ahead.

At a point in the atmosphere where radio signals converge, the sound is mush. We are already at a similar point with information — we are being bombarded by more than we can select or absorb.

How do we sort out truth from error?

How do we discern right from wrong?

How do we bring hope from despair?

Only as we answer these questions can information become knowledge, truth be discerned, and the future be anticipated.

WE ARE IN A CRISIS OF TRUTH.

PART II

MEANING OF MEGATRUTH

MegaTruth is the application of the unchanging Word of God to the new and changing information through the work of the discerning Spirit of Truth.

5.

The Spirit of Truth

Out of the corner of my eye, I caught a glimpse of a game in the window of a Christian bookstore. Bold, black letters on a red box advertised the name of the game: "WORDS OF LIFE — A Game of Biblical Doctrine and Biblical Trivia." The shock of such contradiction stopped me. Curiosity then led me to see what else was being featured as a "leader" in the window to attract customers.

Next to the red box was a white record album with a folksy picture of President Reagan, with two small children at his feet. The title of the album was: "Ronald Reagan Reads Old Testament Bible Stories."

Ah, ha, I thought, *that's great fodder for my weekly radio commentary.*

Completing my shopper's survey of the Christian bookstore window, I laughed as I noted in the company of biblical trivia and Ronald Reagan's reading, a blinking reader board with clip-on letters spelling out:

REGISTER AND VOTE

Healing for Damaged Emotions

$3.69

What a strange connection: A political appeal coupled with a best-selling book by one of our most distinguished professors at Asbury Theological Seminary, Dr. David Seamands. With all due respect to Dr. Seamands, whose book is neither trivia nor hype, there is a somber message in the window of that Christian bookstore.

To me, the game, "Bible Trivia," represents THEOLOGICAL CONFUSION. Have I lost my sense of humor? Isn't biblical trivia a good way to teach the Scriptures? Certainly, there is nothing wrong with an innocent family game. Yet, there is something fundamentally wrong with a trivial approach to the Word of Life. Is it not a fact that churches and Christians are being divided over the authority of Scriptures at the same time that we play games with the Word of God? Like Pogo, we discover we have met the enemy and it is us. It's no wonder that the Word returns to us void; that our energies are consumed in civil warfare; that the media throw Fundamentalists, conservatives, and Evangelicals into the same basket; that we do not challenge the secular mind. As Screwtape said to Wormwood, who was dealing with a patient about to become a Christian, "Do remember that you are there to fuddle him."[1] Theologically, we are fuddled. Something is wrong. What is it?

The album of Ronald Reagan reading Old Testament Bible stories to children represents political contradiction. Certainly there is nothing wrong with a good family record. Yet, something is *fundamentally* wrong. There is an unholy and entangling alliance between conservative Christianity and conservative politics. Evidently, we failed to learn our lesson from those Christians who uncritically embraced the liberal agenda some years ago and now share its bankruptcy. Thus, the prognosis is frightening. Not only will the witness of evangelical Christians be politicized to rise and fall with the fortunes of the Republican Party, but also the witness will be radicalized by extremists who do not distinguish between physical force and righteous anger.

As a case in point, the pro-life movement has spawned a vigilante group called the "Army of God," which justifies protest, harassment, arson and bombing of abortion clinics and family planning agencies. The lunatic fringe? Maybe so. But consider what Francis Schaeffer wrote as the introduction to his chapter entitled, "The Use of Force," in *A Christian Manifesto:*

> There does come a time when force, even physical force, is appropriate. The Christian is not to take the law into his own hands and become a law unto himself. But, when all avenues to flight and protest have closed, force in the defensive posture is appropriate.[2]

Schaeffer's son, Franky, advances his father's thought in his book, *A Time for Anger.* He refers to Acts 5 when Peter was arrested, and we read that the authorities "did not use force because they feared that the people would stone them." In paraphrase of that Scripture for our time, young Schaeffer writes, "they did not use force . . . because their abortion mills [were] burned to the ground and the nation [was] brought to a standstill."[3] Something is wrong. What is it?

Personal chaos is signaled by the need for David Seamands's book, *Healing for Damaged Emotions.* Certainly there is nothing wrong with a book on emotional healing. Yet something is wrong because Christians are such a troubled people. We can understand the emotional buffeting of the secular culture upon the personality, image and identity of the Christian. It is harder to understand the evidence that our emotional problems are relational; presumably relationships are to be the point of our strength. Eighty percent of the books sold in Christian bookstores deal with personal and interpersonal problems. One out of three ministerial marriages is breaking up. If the trend continues, divorce among ministerial couples by the turn of the century

will hit one of two marriages, equaling the current ratio in the
society at large.

As an observer of the contemporary religious scene, I see
our personal chaos being worked out in a variety of extremes.
In one corner is the cluster of Christians known as "Orthodox
Evangelicals." Led by people who made up the Jesus movement
in the late 1960s, they have ridden the pendulum from free-form
religion to its opposite expression — a highly-structured orthodoxy, liturgy and authority. A young convert to orthodox
evangelicalism with whom I counseled could not sign a contract,
pursue a degree, buy a home, or make an investment without
the permission of his bishop. In another corner there are the
"Worldly Evangelicals" identified by Quebedeaux in his book
by that title.[4] These people tend to be former fundamentalists,
he says, who have rejected the rigidity of their past with its
five "Fundy" sins — smoking, drinking, dancing, card-playing,
and movies. What used to be sin is now subsumed under the
category of "style." With their new-found freedom from past
strictures, the Worldly Evangelicals assume an openness to
intellect, an opposition to institutionalized authority, an attention
to social issues, and an alignment with liberal causes.

Someplace between is a category called "Charismatic
Evangelicals." For them, the baptism of the Holy Spirit and
the attendant gifts or "charismata," with emphasis upon healing,
prophecy, and tongues, are the evidence of spirituality. In
contrast with the classical Pentecostals of the past, Charismatic
Evangelicals tend to be middle- and upper-middle-class Christians who remain in established churches with a dedication to
spiritual renewal. The problem is that experience takes precedence over doctrine, thus tending toward an authority based
upon personal, and often faulty, biblical exegesis. Experience
also takes precedence over reason, thus contributing to the air
of anti-intellectualism in evangelical ranks. Something is wrong.
What is it?

Floating almost free from evangelical definition is another
group of contemporary Christians whom I call "Invisible
Evangelicals." George Gallup, Jr., in his book, *The Search for*

America's Faith, relates his discovery of a group of people who
are evangelical in belief, but invisible in identity.[5] Many are
faceless numbers of the electronic church, but many have no
connection at all. Martin Marty describes these people as
Christian products of the consumer society. They pick and
choose among the offerings of the bookstore, the television
set, the magazine rack and the promptings of the heart. They
find meaning without belonging, religion without community.

> Personal religion is chosen by millions as an alterna-
> tive to religionlessness or godlessness.

> The religion of the high-rise apartment and the long
> weekend is likely to grow and be an ever more
> confusing alternative to church membership than
> anti-religion or mere secularity ever was.[6]

Something is wrong. What is it?

THE CRISIS OF TRUTH IS WITHIN THE CHURCH
AS WELL AS IN THE SOCIETY.

Blamires, in the introduction to his book, *Where Do We
Stand?* writes,

> Today's boundary between Christian fidelity and
> treachery is not a floodlit Berlin wall, set about with
> watchtowers and man-traps and patrolled by jealous
> guardsmen; it is a frontier barely recognizable on
> the terrain over which it runs.[7]

To locate the frontier, Blamires says that we must engage
in map work, charting the terrain and drawing the dividing line
between faithful Christian witness and apostasy. His analogy
of our task as map work is good. It goes beyond the demand
for a rule book of "proof texts," which requires no discerning
judgment in moral decisions. At a recent board meeting of a
Christian publishing house, we reviewed the best-selling books
in the evangelical market and observed that if the faith can be
reduced to formulas for lay people and alliterative outlines for

preachers, sales are guaranteed. A map is better than a rule book for guiding Christians through the no man's land of a changing, secular society. The fact is that we have that map in the Word of God. We believe it is the "only infallible rule for life and faith" (Lausanne Covenant) in every generation and in all circumstances. Yet, according to the promise of Christ, it is the work of the Holy Spirit to trace the map of revelation for the new frontiers of Christian fidelity and witness in each generation.

WE NEED THE GYROSCOPE OF THE HOLY SPIRIT TO KEEP US ON CENTER AND HEADING IN THE RIGHT DIRECTION.

Jesus anticipated the crisis of truth in the coming Age of Information when He promised that "when he, the Spirit of truth, is come, he will guide you into all truth"; "he will reprove [convict] the world of sin, and of righteousness, and of judgment"; and, "he will shew you things to come" (John 16:13 and 8).

We have emphasized the role of the Holy Spirit as our sanctifying, comforting, enhancing, empowering and equipping presence. We have not fully considered His primary role as the Spirit of Truth.

Futurists tell us that if we are prepared to live in the world of tomorrow, we must be taught the processes of *synthesizing, norming,* and *futuring.* How providential! Synthesizing is the integration of new information and changing life circumstances into our working world view. Is not this what Jesus means when He promises that the Holy Spirit will "lead us into all truth"? Norming is the process of setting moral standards for running the mazeways of a changing society. Is not this what Jesus means when He promises that the Holy Spirit will convict the world of sin, righteousness, and judgment? Futuring is the task of developing a long-term view of our destiny. Is not this what Jesus means when He promises that the Holy Spirit will "show us things to come"?

WITH THE WORD OF GOD AS OUR TEXT
AND THE HOLY SPIRIT AS OUR TEACHER,
WE CAN KNOW HI/TRUTH IN A HI/TECH AGE.

We have seen a direct connection between the futurist's educational task and the Holy Spirit's teaching role. Together, they constitute the creation of a Christian world view. According to Kenneth Boulding in his book, *The Meaning of the Twentieth Century: The Great Transition,* a world view has three parts:

> *An interpretation of human history* that unfolds before us as convincing drama in which we find our role;

> *A moral standard or system of values* by which to judge truth and error in our human knowledge, good and evil in our human behavior; and

> *A vision of the future* that is significant, exciting and positive, and in which we see our part.[8]

To explore the full potential of these promises in the Age of Information is to come to *MegaTruth.* We need a Christian world view through which to see the meaning of *Megatrends.*

6.

The Synthesizing Spirit

Gerald Ford, our former president, loved to tell the story about the minister who paid a pastoral call on a farmer. As they sat on the farmer's porch, the minister looked out to a hillside where a forest fire had burned away all the foliage and vegetation. Noting a new stand of scrub brush poking through the blackened soil, the minister commented, "It's not very attractive, is it?"

"You're right," the farmer answered, "it's not as pretty as it could be, but it holds the world together."

Naisbitt's unsettling observation comes back to us: "We are drowning in information, but starving for knowledge." Our own question returns to us: How do we organize the mass of new and changing information to make it meaningful? In other words,

HOW DO WE HOLD OUR WORLD TOGETHER IN THE AGE OF INFORMATION?

The futurist's task of synthesizing and the philosopher's interpretation of the meaning of human history come together in Jesus' promise that the Holy Spirit will "lead you into all truth." In the Christian world view, the drama of human history is interpreted by the incarnation of God in Jesus Christ for the redemption of humankind. "All truth" is the promise of a world view that embraces the whole of life. But to be whole, a world view must have a center. Therefore, the Christian world view is focused upon the person of Jesus Christ. As C. S. Lewis said, Jesus Christ must be our "overwhelming first." No one else can be at the center. This fact is reinforced by Jesus' word that even the Holy Spirit will not speak of Himself, but only of what He has heard Christ speak. He shows us only what Christ has shown Him and He leads us only into the truth that Christ has revealed to Him.

OUR CHRISTIAN WORLD VIEW
IN THE AGE OF INFORMATION
MUST BE CENTERED IN CHRIST.

Two dangers persist in the contemporary scene which distort the focus on Jesus Christ as the center and create a lopsided Christian world view. One danger is *fragmentation of the faith* by overemphasizing a single doctrine. There is a tendency among evangelical Christians to elevate some aspect of Christian belief to the level of a litmus test for the faith, or a panacea for spiritual problems. The danger is in narrowing such all-important issues as the authority of Scriptures or the sanctity of life into personal or political dogmas that cut off debate and break Christian fellowship.

Similar concerns can be expressed over theological emphases which raise a cardinal doctrine such as the creation, fall, incarnation, resurrection, or second coming to an overbalanced position. In my Wesleyan tradition, for instance, we have been guilty of narrowing the biblical experience of the Spirit-filled life into a doctrine that has lost its dynamic in the confusion with "perfectionism." With deep regret, I see evangelical Christianity wobbling between extremes on the doctrine and experience of the Holy Spirit. Prominent theologians out of the Reformed traditions are identified as spokesmen for evangelical Christianity. Yet, because of their reaction against "holiness," their writings are weak on the Holy Spirit as a work of grace.

No wonder, then, that the charismatic movement has stolen the day. The symptoms of theological confusion, political contradiction, emotional excesses, and moral chaos which plague our evangelical house can be traced directly to our deficient doctrine of the Holy Spirit. It is not too late. The new generation of Wesleyan and Reformed theologians needs to sit down in a summit meeting on the work of the Holy Spirit with the goal of restoring dynamic balance between its biblical doctrine and the personal experience of the "Spirit of Truth."

There is always the danger of the fragmentation of the faith by an overemphasis upon some facet of Christian doctrine. We need to remember Jesus Christ is the single subject for our confession of faith and the single center for our Christian world view. As Paul writes to the Corinthians, "No man can say that Jesus is the Lord, but by the Holy Ghost" (1 Corinthians 12:3). As the chaplain for Clemson University said in an ecumenical worship service of many Christian groups, "We may say more, but we cannot say less." Only as the Holy Spirit becomes the gyroscope to keep us in balance among the cardinal doctrines will we have a whole world view that is centered in Jesus Christ.

Compartmentalization of our conduct is the second danger to a Christ-centered, whole-world perspective. Gordon Allport, the Harvard psychologist, did a study of persons who professed Jesus Christ as the central and controlling figure in their lives. He found that people holding a common profession of Christ acted in two different ways. One group acted consistently with their profession while the other group participated in contradictory acts. Studying the two groups in depth, Allport concluded that there was a difference between *intrinsic centering* and *extrinsic centering.*[1] Those who acted consistently with their profession held Jesus Christ intrinsically at the center of their souls. Naturally, then, their behavior in all of life was consistent with the Spirit of Jesus Christ. Those who acted inconsistently with the profession of faith, however, were found to have contaminating elements competing for control of their world view and their behavior. Realistically, their profession of Christ was pushed out of the center by these competing demands.

Allport's study reinforces the warning of James that "a double minded man is unstable in all his ways" (James 1:8).

Much attention is being given today to the collision between the Christian and the secular world views. I agree with Blamires who says that we cannot compromise with a secular world view assuming that down the road we may have a fender-bender with our faith.[2] Christian and secular world views are on a collision course which will result in a total wreck for one or the other. Not enough attention, however, has been given to the contamination at the center of our faith through the secular attitude of self-interest. The conflict does not rage along a well-defined Maginot Line. Rather, like the Viet Nam struggle, the enemy is engaged in guerilla warfare and soldiers cannot be distinguished from citizens. Under the contamination of self-interest, our economics become self-indulgent, our politics become self-protective, our psychology becomes self-enhancing, and our theology becomes self-pitying. Silently and surreptitiously, we are conquered by contamination at the core of our spiritual being. Only the continuing presence and cleansing power of the Holy Spirit can keep us intrinsically centered in Jesus Christ. If we are to see truth whole in the Age of Information, Jesus Christ must be the substantive and singular center of our soul.

OUR CHRISTIAN WORLD VIEW
IN THE AGE OF INFORMATION
MUST BE COMPREHENSIVE.

Jesus promises us that the Holy Spirit will lead us into *all* truth. James Orr, in his classic work, *The Christian View of God and the World,* says that when we make our commitment to the centrality of Jesus Christ, we commit ourselves to a lot more besides.[3] We commit ourselves to the Bible as the revelation of the nature of God, the interpretation of human history, and the prediction of human destiny. We commit ourselves to the mind of Christ. Blamires in his book, *The Christian Mind,* says that we will have supernatural orientation through which we see God at work in our world today through His transcendent power.[4] We will have a view of human nature that sees the reality of sin. We will have a sense of truth in which we hold in balance the doctrines of creation, the fall, the incarnation, the resurrection, and the second coming. We will submit to the authority of the Word of God for the direction of our lives. Paul sums up the comprehensive nature of our Christian world view when he writes:

> In Him all things hold together (Colossians 1:17 RSV).

Therefore, there are no advances in human knowledge or events in human history that are excluded from our comprehensive world view.

When I was a college freshman, my first course in theology was taught by Dr. James Gregory. To describe the work of the Holy Spirit in our lives, he took a thread from his blue suit and said, "If you take any thread from this suit and put it under a microscope, you will see that it has the tone and the texture of the whole cloth." Then he applied his analogy: "That's how the Holy Spirit fills our lives. Every fiber of our being is comprehensively and consistently pervaded by the tone and texture of the Spirit-filled life." The same can be said for our Christian world view. When Jesus promises that the Spirit will "lead you into all truth," He means that there are no facts, ideas, notions, values or opinions that are not made "captive to the mind of Christ" by the Spirit of Truth.

OUR CHRISTIAN WORLD VIEW
IN THE AGE OF INFORMATION
MUST BE CREATIVE.

Even though our Christian world view is created around the centrality of Christ, and is comprehensive, it does not mean that we have all the answers or are exempt from surprise. To the contrary, our Christian world view is continuously being recreated as the Holy Spirit teaches us how to process new information through spiritual discernment. Bernard Ramm, the theologian, suggests that new information coming into our field of experience may be processed in one of three ways. If the information is compatible with the Word of God, we integrate it into our Christian world view. If it conflicts with the Word of God, we reject it as part of our world view and refute it with reasoned understanding. But if the new information is a mystery which is neither compatible nor conflicting with our Christian world view, we hold it in abeyance as an "imponderable" which invites further investigation. In each case, the Holy Spirit is our teacher, helping us discern how new information is related to our Christian world view.

The danger is *closure*. As new information is introduced to us, we are tempted to close the circle of our Christian world view and stop growing. We must remember that Christianity is the only world view that does not have to close the circle. Our faith lets us be fallible. We can admit that we do not have all the answers, but we know the God who is the source of all truth. Human systems do not have the privilege of faith for their imponderables. Whether in science, philosophy or religion, human systems must close the circle of knowledge. Science, for instance, has as its avowed goal the prediction and control of all aspects of physical and human nature through the discoveries of the empirical process. Scientists are driven by both frustration and anticipation in their research as they seek to close the circle.

Recently, a telescope the size of a bus was launched into space. From its orbiting position, the spacescope will be able to see clearly through twelve billion light-years of the universe. The assumption is that scientists will be able to view 85 percent of the universe and come closer to determining its origin and its destiny. Of course, the scientists also are assuming that the universe is finite rather than eternal, and natural rather than supernatural. They are driven to close the circle.

Back on earth, we have the example of B. F. Skinner, the well-known exponent of classical conditioning in psychology. At the center of his theory is the assumption that all human behavior can be predicted and controlled by the behavioristic formula of stimulus and response. In other words, he extends the experiment with Pavlov's dog into a comprehensive world view. Skinner's novel, *Walden II,* creates a utopian world in which all human behavior is conditioned by that mechanism of stimulus and response. At the close of the novel, Frazer, who is the mastermind of Walden II, stands high upon a bluff musing with satisfaction over the perfect world that he has created. Skinner, then, reveals his nihilistic theology when he writes his last sentence:

> Frazer's not on his throne,
> all's right with the world.[5]

Because Skinner's world has neither transcendent dimensions nor eternal scope, he must close his world view around a self-perpetuating behaviorism which becomes a god in itself.

My son, Rob, just completed a book report on George Orwell's *Nineteen Eighty-Four.*[6] Like Skinner, Orwell created a utopian world based upon a closed, totalitarian system. In Orwell's fantasy, however, one person, who stands in opposition to the system, threatens to bring down the utopian world. All human dictatorships are vulnerable to the same threat. In the Philippines, the dictator Marcos could not tolerate the opposition of an Acquino. Likewise, in South Africa, the totalitarian system of apartheid must have martial law to still the dissident voice.

Our Christian world is not threatened by the anxiety of new information or the intolerance of personal protest. With the promise that the Holy Spirit will "lead" us into all truth, we know that truth is progressive and our understanding is developmental. Along a line of continuous and creative teaching, the Holy Spirit brings us the truth when we need it and when we are ready for it. Thus, in the struggle with new information, changing circumstances and critical opposition, we have the potential for spiritual growth.

The Book of Job holds an example of *closure* versus *creativity.* Eliphaz, Bildad and Zophar were the victims of a world view that is closed in by human reason and religious tradition. Simply stated, they had reduced religion to the formula that equates suffering with sin, and prosperity with righteousness. In their view, all of human history can be interpreted according to this scheme. Suddenly, their esteemed friend Job — a man whose righeousness is rewarded by health, wealth, family and fame — confronts circumstances that threaten their formula. Job suffers the loss of all but his life. According to the formula, it means that he has sinned. Yet, in the midst of his suffering, Job contends for his innocence. The contradiction is more than his three friends can handle. Relentlessly and without mercy, they probe for the sin in his life. Pretending to defend God, they defend themselves by closing the circle of their rigid system and condemning Job without proving his sin. Job, however, holds his faith in God while struggling with the contradiction. He never gets an answer to the reason for his suffering, but he breaks through to a new level of faith when he sees who God is and submits himself to His good, though unknown, purpose.

Job is a hero of faith whose suffering teaches us how the Holy Spirit will lead us creatively into all truth as we encounter new information, changing circumstances and critical opposition in the coming Age of Information.

THROUGH THE SYNTHESIZING SPIRIT OF TRUTH, CHRISTIANS CAN LIVE WITH MEANING IN THE AGE OF INFORMATION.

7.

The Norming Spirit

A psychiatrist who specialized in the study of sexual behavior took as the subject for an address at a Rotary Club, "The Sexual Revolution Is Over. Now What?" He cited information showing how our attitudes toward sex had turned upside-down during the 1960s and 1970s. A majority of Americans who were shocked by pre-marital sex, cohabitation, extra-marital affairs and homosexuality came to accept these behaviors as matters of personal preference, not social morality. To deal with these changing attitudes toward sex, the psychiatrist proposed that the Wolfenden Report, done in Britain by the Church of England, serve as the model for a new moral standard. Simply put, the measure of morality would be, "Whatever is done in private by consenting adults is not a matter of public morality." In support of that position, the speaker added the thought that the pluralism which guides religious freedom should now apply to sexual choice. "You go to your church and I'll go to mine" becomes "You do your sex and I'll do mine."

No wonder morality today has been compared to playing baseball with a movable left field fence. Yesterday's home runs become today's easy outs.

WHAT IS THE MORAL STANDARD FOR THE CHURCH
IN THE AGE OF INFORMATION?

New information is not morally neutral. The more information we have, the more complex is the moral decision we must make. In the coming Age of Information, Naisbitt foresees us moving from a simple world of either/or choices to a complex world of multiple options. With fitting analogy, he remembers the time when we had a choice of vanilla or chocolate ice cream, and compares that choice with the thirty-one flavors now offered by Baskin-Robbins ice cream parlors. A recent newspaper article told of the dilemma of a Russian defector who won asylum in the United States. He said he wanted to go back to Russia because he could not handle the number of free choices required of him in America. The forced choice of either/or decisions under communism was preferable to the multiple options which he encountered in our democracy.

If we are honest, we will admit that we, too, prefer the simple world of either/or choices in our faith. Humankind seems to have two counterbalancing needs — to be free and to be secure at the same time. When we are free, we want to be secure; and when we are secure, we want to be free. Perhaps that is why our extensive freedom in the United States today leads us to seek the security of a standard of ethics that is true or false, black or white. New information that requires a moral decision, then, can be processed into a forced-choice category with biblical justification. Abortion is an example. If the issue is simplified as an either/or decision, all of the mitigating factors, such as rape of a minor child or incest, have to be ignored or subjected to the higher principle of the sanctity of life. New information relating to the conception and continuation of life must be processed the same way. To be consistent, we who advocate a pro-life position must deal with the pre-life issues of contraception, in vitro conception, genetic research, and biotechnology. Our responsibility continues into the social issues of adoption, health care, hunger, education and employment, which are created when we choose the alternative to abortion. Nor can we avoid the moral consequences of a pro-life decision at the *end* of life — the physical, mental, emotional, economic and relational consequences of prolonging life through medical advancements.

Sooner or later, we will have to recognize that not all the moral issues coming at us from the Age of Information lend themselves to either/or decisions. New information will reveal complexities, contingencies and consequences that will give multiple options to our moral decisions. Rather than simply sorting our choices into either/or categories, we will have to work along an ethical continuum which requires that we consider the options, anticipate the connectors, and weigh the consequences of our decisions. The burden will be too heavy for our minds unless we have the discerning mind of the Spirit of Truth. Jesus anticipates our need in His promise,

> And when He [the Spirit of Truth] has come, He
> will convict the world of sin, and of righteousness,
> and of judgment: of sin, because they do not believe
> in Me; of righteousness, because I go to My Father
> and you see Me no more; of judgment, because the
> ruler of this world is judged (John 16:8, NKJV).

In this promise are the components for a system of values and a standard for moral decisions that are essential for the Christian world view. An ethical system requires three parts: a *standard* by which to judge right and wrong, a *sanction* that affirms right and condemns wrong, and a *consequence* which rewards right and punishes wrong.

The change in public attitude toward premarital sex illustrates how an ethical system works — and how it breaks down. Not many years ago there was the *standard,* supported by consensus, that premarital sex was wrong. Public opinion confirmed the standard by *sanctions* which affirmed young people who deferred sex until marriage and condemned those who failed to live up to the standard. *Consequences* sealed the ethical system. Young people who participated in premarital sex lived with the fear of pregnancy, and those who became pregnant served as examples of the consequences of the broken standard. Then, in the

1960s, the standard was challenged by the Kinsey Report, the sanctions were left behind when the automobile made our society increasingly mobile, and the consequences were lifted by the "pill." Today, in the public mind, premarital sex is accepted as individual preference without social condemnation and without the fear of pregnancy. An ethical system has broken down.

A vital function of the Holy Spirit is to maintain the spiritual values revealed in Jesus Christ which are essential to our Christian world view. In the task of convicting the world of sin, righteousness and judgment, the Spirit reveals the standard, sanctions, and consequences by which we are to judge right and wrong in human behavior and make our moral decisions.

OUR MORAL STANDARD IS BELIEF IN JESUS CHRIST.

Sin is defined as the failure to believe in Jesus Christ. Behind that standard is the fact that human nature is in rebellion against God as evidenced by the rejection of Jesus Christ. The Holy Spirit's task is to convict the world of its sin and remind Christians that there is no other standard by which faith is judged. As Charles Wesley, with his gift for putting truth into song, writes,

> I want a principle within of watchful, godly fear
> A sensibility of sin, a pain to feel it near,
> Help me the first approach to feel of pride or wrong
>   desire,
> To catch the wandering of my will and quench the
>   kindling fire.

To invoke belief in Jesus Christ as the moral standard for Christian ethics may seem like carrying coals to Newcastle. But then, we remember that Kierkegaard once wrote, "If the Word of God said that everyone who believed was to receive a $100,000 gift, there would be no doubt about the clarity of the revelation and the promise." There would be no need for theologians to debate this truth, no need for commentaries to interpret it, and no need for seminaries to teach it. Everyone would believe the Word at face value. But perhaps with tongue in cheek, Kierkegaard notes, "The Word says with equal clarity that Jesus is Lord and there is no redemption other than in Him." So, he says, "We establish theologians to study it . . . commentaries to interpret it and . . . seminaries to teach it." With Kierkegaard, we have to wonder if we really accept the fact of Jesus Christ as the moral standard against which all human behavior is judged, or do we hope that our theologians, commentaries and seminaries might find that this truth is not quite true or at least that it is not demanded of us?[1] The work of the Holy Spirit is to press upon us the fact that our human nature is sinful and our only hope is belief in Jesus Christ.

Every moral decision, then, must be weighed against this standard. The temptation is to modify our position on the sinfulness of human nature and extend the hope for salvation beyond belief in Jesus Christ. When one prominent television preacher heard a fellow evangelist declare that the gospel of Jesus Christ still cuts through to convict the heart of the sinner, he walked out of the service saying that we cannot reach the people of our age with a message of sin. Likewise, in a review of the counseling theory of Carl Rogers, *Christianity Today* notes that evangelical Christians tend to accept uncritically non-directive therapy which assumes that human nature has within itself the resources for healing and maturity without the grace of God.[2]

As we noted earlier, Naisbitt himself is guilty of assuming that the rising consciousness of human nature and the upward momentum of social change will transform our society. He fails the first test of Christian ethics. Whether dealing with facts or opinions, ideas or values, theory or practice which come to us from the Age of Information, our first question must be, What is the moral standard upon which our decision is based? The Holy Spirit will convict us if we fail to recognize that sin is to believe in someone or something other than Jesus Christ for our salvation.

OUR MORAL SANCTION IS RIGHTEOUSNESS THROUGH JESUS CHRIST.

The second moral function of the Spirit of Truth is to convict the world of the meaning of righteousness. As always, the focus is on Jesus Christ who says that He is going to His Father and we will see Him no more. Yet, through the agency of the Holy Spirit, He leaves us the image of righteousness. Thus, our Christian ethic teaches us what is right and what is wrong. Fundamentally, we know that we have no righteousness of our own. Only as the Holy Spirit leads us to faith in Jesus Christ are we redeemed. The good news is that the gospel does not leave us wallowing in the slough of our depravity. Against that despair, John Wesley saw the doctrine of "prevenient grace." With the Calvinists, he acknowledged that sin so pervades our being that we are incapable of responding to God within ourselves. But the Holy Spirit comes to us with the awakening grace that precedes redeeming grace. He not only convicts us of our sin but He shows us the hope of righteousness in Jesus Christ.

If I were asked to name the ten books that have had the most influence on my life, I would put close to the top of the list Charles Sheldon's novel, *In His Steps.* As a teen-ager seeking to know the will of God, I shall never forget the question that the characters in the book chose as the guide for their decisions: What would Jesus do? Time and time again, I have asked that question when confronted with decisions, large and small. Without fail, the question has taken me deeply into the mind and spirit of Jesus Christ. More often than not, the Holy Spirit brings from my memory an event or teaching from the life of Jesus which becomes a meaningful guide for my decision.

I saw this truth in action for someone else, too. A prominent judge sat with us in a prayer breakfast in which we spoke of our needs, sought guidance from the Word, and prayed for each other. In his turn, he told about the case of a woman who had been tried for a minor crime and found innocent. She then brought suit to have her police record cleared. The judge had heard the case and had to make a decision that day. In the course of our scriptural study, we read the story of the woman taken in adultery. After her accusers had slunk away under the condemnation of their own sin, Jesus asked the woman, "Who is it that accuses you?"

When she looked around and answered, "No man, Lord," He pronounced His verdict, "Neither do I condemn you; go and sin no more."

Hearing those words, the judge said, "I know what my decision will be. Her record will be wiped clean." By learning what Jesus did, he knew what he must do.

Therefore, the second question that the Holy Spirit will bring to our mind in the midst of moral decision-making is: What would Jesus do? His righteousness is our righteousness.

OUR MORAL CONSEQUENCE IS JUDGMENT BY JESUS CHRIST.

The Spirit of Truth will convict the world of judgment "because the ruler of this world is judged." We must be reminded constantly that all mankind is accountable to God. The cross of Jesus Christ is the symbol of His judgment upon sin and Satan. In the cross there is full freedom from the condemnation of sin, but there is also the continuing judgment upon the works and the ways of men.

In *Megatrends,* Naisbitt gives us no standard for judging the ten trends that are transforming our society other than obsolescence if we fail to ride with the trends. Our Christian world view, however, has a qualitative, spiritual standard against which to judge the trends. If the trends are moving to condone sin, whether in situational ethics or neglect of the poor, the cross will stand in judgment. We already have referred to the megashift from either/or to multiple options in our choices of lifestyle based upon new information. Naisbitt includes multiple options for marriage, family, work and religion along with ice cream, automobiles and entertainment. He makes no moral distinction, however, for the sanctity of marriage, the stability of the family, the vocation of work or the theology of religion. In each of these cases, the cross of Jesus Christ stands in the way as the symbol of judgment. For non-believers, the cross is still a scandal which impales them on their sin. For believers, the cross is still the symbol before which we bow to confess our sins and from which we rise to serve God with gratitude and humility.

The Holy Spirit saves us from arrogance by reminding us that all of our works, Christian or secular, will be judged. New information brings with it the temptation to assume that we are becoming smarter and wiser. A comic came close to the truth when he said, "We know more and more about less and less. Soon we will know everything about nothing." The evidence is against us. Advancements in human knowledge do not automatically bring new meaning to our lives or morality to our decisions. Rather, new knowledge accentuates the need for wisdom beyond human capacity in order to avoid disaster. It is the function of the Spirit of Truth to keep us humble by reminding us that our human achievements are incomplete and often in error. For example, physical science was revolutionized by Galileo's theory of gravity which included the principle of equivalence — meaning that a feather and a rock would fall at the same rate of acceleration in a vacuum. Suddenly, sophisticated advancements in research instruments are making it possible to refine the testing of falling objects with the result that Galileo's theory of gravity and even Einstein's theory of relativity are coming into question. Natural law has a way of keeping scientists humble.

Christians who believe that they are doing the work and will of God especially need humility. Our best efforts are usually flawed by mixed motives and limited understanding. We, too, stand under the judgment of God. Therefore, the Holy Spirit will not let us take ourselves too seriously. In fact, I believe that one of the signs of the Spirit-filled life is the ability to laugh at yourself. Karl Barth is known as the "laughing theologian." His attitude is in sharp contrast to the person who said, "I wanted to be a theologian, but cheerfulness kept creeping in." Frankly, I am suspicious of persons who are so convinced in their faith or so compelled in their ministry that they cannot laugh.

Robert Webber says Evangelicals in this generation act as if we have stepped off the pages of Scripture to do the work of Acts all over again. "Be not wise in your own conceits" is a timely reminder from the apostle Paul which the Holy Spirit brings to our mind. Not only is the ruler of this world judged by the cross of Jesus Christ, but the Holy Spirit will not let our works of righteousness make us wise in our own conceits.

Our moral decisions in an Age of Information will be subject to the same convicting presence of the Holy Spirit. He will not only keep before us the standard and the sanction of right and wrong, but He will help us consider the consequences of our choices.

THROUGH THE NORMING SPIRIT OF TRUTH, CHRISTIANS CAN LIVE MORALLY IN THE AGE OF INFORMATION.

8.

The Futuring Spirit

Young, well-educated and affluent adults were asked in a nation-wide poll about their attitudes toward the future. The typical interview went like this:

> *Question:* Do you feel as if the future will
> be better or worse than today?
>
> *Answer:* Worse.
>
> *Question:* Then, you must despair of the future?
>
> *Answer:* Oh, no.
>
> *Question:* Why not?
>
> *Answer:* Because I intend to have a good job, a
> good salary and a good life.

Contradiction glares at us. How can personal hope for the future be disengaged from despair for the society? A strange mixture of optimism and pessimism, especially among the young, bodes trouble for tomorrow. Lest we become victims of the same confusion, we must ask,

WHAT IS THE VISION OF HOPE FOR THE CHURCH IN THE AGE OF INFORMATION?

Our Christian world view must include a significant and exciting vision of the future in which we find our part. Jesus promises to give us that vision through the work of the Holy Spirit Who will "show you things to come." We are now in a minefield set with apocalyptic, eschatological and teleological traps. Yet, we know that the way in which we look forward to the future and view the end of time determines our daily attitudes and actions. Only the Holy Spirit can help us work our way through the minefield and draw a map for others to follow.

Let's return to our analogy of the Holy Spirit as our gyroscope. He balances, first of all, our *short-term* with our *long-term* view of the future. Naisbitt tells us that the more information we have upon which to project the future, the greater will be the resulting megashift from short-term to long-term planning. This is only partially true. Naisbitt admits that the short-term demand for profits may counter long-term planning which requires the deferral of immediate returns. This is about as close as he comes to admitting the selfishness of human nature. In the secular society, the pendulum always swings between immediate gratification and long-term benefits. The oil crisis of the mid-1970s illustrates our inconsistency. After the warning that our oil resources were being depleted, economic and political interests created the crisis. We panicked at the gas pump. But then when prices were doubled and an oil glut was announced, we canceled our national drive for the conservation of resources and returned to our wasteful habits. Today, little or no attention is being paid to the facts which predict a valid crisis for future generations unless we conserve our current energy and develop new resources.

Christians are motivated and guided by the long-term goal of the Great Commission. To preach, teach and disciple the people of all nations is our vision for the future. It requires both a sense of urgency for the present and planning with foresight for the future. But strategic planning to implement the vision of the Great Commission is rare in the church. In many instances, tactics which produce numbers, dollars, programs, popularity, and power have taken over our ministries. Long-range planning is a popular exercise that is often initiated but seldom implemented.

The Holy Spirit will balance our tendency to vacillate between short-term results and long-term planning through the means of a "strategic vision" of the future.

Not long ago we thought that effective leaders outlined their vision for the future in detailed steps as far as five years in advance. Now we know differently. Detailed long-range plans tend to paralyze leadership into place. Once a five-year plan is announced, for instance, no one forgets it. Even though it is only a plan with provision for annual adjustments, its ink becomes an iron rule. If circumstances change and the plan is revised, the credibility of leadership is called into question.

A strategic vision, however, avoids the pitfalls of both short-term expediency and long-term idealism. Effective leaders who exercise a strategic vision have a detailed plan for immediate short-range action, but as you probe their thoughts for the future, the details blur and give way to their vision which becomes clearer than ever. Others who demand details for the future will be frustrated by the relaxed, even playful, attitude with which these leaders relate to the future. A story, a joke, an anecdote may seem irrelevant, but in truth the leader is communicating his vision for the future and is engaging others in its meaning. When Jesus promises that the Spirit of Truth will show us things to come, He does not indicate we should expect details of a long-range plan dictating every step. Rather, in fulfillment of the proverb, "A man's heart plans his way, but the Lord directs his steps" (Proverbs 16:9), the Holy Spirit balances our view of the future with short-term steps and a long-term vision. He shows us how to lead productively, playfully and purposefully.

Second, the Holy Spirit balances our *pessimism* and our *optimism* when He shows us things to come. Futurists vary from giddy optimists to fatalistic pessimists. If their projections are based upon a philosophy of life that is wholly optimistic, a euphoric approach to a utopian future follows. Most often, however, utopias are foreseen in novels, dramas and science fiction fantasies. The current craze for such movies as "Superman," "Star Wars," and "Back to the Future" is symptomatic of our human desire to fashion our fear of the future into a world in which everything comes out right. An in-depth analysis of these films reveals theological undertones, but usually there is a god without personality and redemption without atonement.

Futurists who are closer to the facts tend to lurch toward the other extreme. A wave of futuristic interest in the 1970s grew out of the much-maligned report from the Club of Rome which predicted ecological catastrophe if we wasted our limited resources while polluting our environment. Although the predictions have been contested, they have not been refuted. Naisbitt may be right when he says that a society can deal with only one issue at a time. After the scares of a poisoned environment, we had temporary fits of anger while waiting in gas lines. Then, one by one, our pessimistic concerns faded. We made a weak attempt to institute a national "Earth Day," yawned at Gerald Ford's "W.I.N." buttons, and laughed at Jimmy Carter's "cardigan sweater" economy in a cold White House. Today, most of us have reverted to our gas-guzzling, air-polluting, energy-wasting ways.

OUR "COWBOY ECONOMY" RIDES AGAIN!

Riding the crest of our alternative hopes and fears for the future are a host of popular authors who walk the line between optimism and pessimism, utopia and catastrophe, and perhaps between science and fiction. Alvin Toffler is the best known of these authors. His best-selling works, *Future Shock* and *The Third Wave*, are secular prophecies written with evangelistic fervor and popularized by journalistic code words, such as "ecocatastrophe," which rouse our attention and awaken our guilt. By and large, futurists such as Toffler hinge their optimism or pessimism upon an idealistic *if*. They see hope for the future only *if* we repent of our ecological sins, turn from our wasteful ways and believe the gospel of environmental protection and economic redistribution.

Only the Holy Spirit can save us from the ups of giddy optimism and the downs of fatalistic pessimism. Like a gyroscope whose stability increases with speed, the Holy Spirit gives us the balance of peace, joy and love at the center of our souls even when the moods of society are spinning wildly almost out of control.

Third, the Holy Spirit balances *process* and *event* for our future. Christians invariably struggle with the meaning of time as it relates to the future. Postmillennialists tend to emphasize the ongoing process of bringing in the Kingdom of God; premillennialists tend to downplay process in favor of the event of the second coming; and amillennialists want to neutralize the timing for both process and event. Danger lurks within each option. Those who are given to process can become embroiled in various forms of "process theology" which permits an easy takeover by political philosophies because they lack disciplined accountability to the imminent return of Jesus Christ. Conversely, those who fix upon the event of Jesus' return become absorbed with dispensations and dates, draining off energy from ongoing ministry. Sad to say, those who make the future timeless tend to lose both the patience of the process and the expectation of the event. Jacques Elul in *The Meaning of the City* seems to find the equilibrium of the Spirit of Truth when he says that we must work for the redemption of the city while being prepared to flee from the wrath to come at any time.[1]

Thus, we have come full cycle to the truth that our task as stewards of Christ is to obey His command, "Occupy till I come." Fully invested and fully alive in the present moment, we never lose sight of the purpose for which we work — the grandest event of all, when He "shall come in the glory of his Father with his angels; and then he shall reward every man according to his works" (Matthew 16:27).

**THROUGH THE FUTURING SPIRIT OF TRUTH,
CHRISTIANS CAN LIVE WITH EXPECTANT HOPE
IN THE AGE OF INFORMATION.**

9.

The Engaging Spirit

Earlier, we posed the question, What is the business of the church in the Age of Information? We now have the answer. Through the work of the synthesizing, norming and futuring Spirit of Truth, our business is to create and communicate the Christian world view in which

all *history* is interpreted by the provision of Jesus Christ;

all *humanity* is judged by the person of Jesus Christ; and

all *hope* is foreseen in the promise of Jesus Christ.

To summarize our thoughts, the following chart shows our dilemmas in the Age of Information, our tasks for teaching and learning, our need for a world view, our promise of the Spirit of Truth and our goal for MegaTruth — a Christian world view. The chart is still incomplete. As a theoretical framework, it is like a skeleton without flesh and blood. If the Christian world view is no more than an intellectual construct, it means that we have split the personality of the Holy Spirit into a

89

MEGATRUTH FOR THE AGE OF INFORMATION

Our Dilemmas in the Age of Information	Our Tasks for teaching and learning	Our Framework for a world view	Our Promise "When He, the Spirit of Truth is come, He	Our Goal for MegaTruth: the Christian world view
Information overload: "How do we sort out truth from error?"	Synthesizing	A significant interpretation of the meaning of history in which we have our role	. . . will lead you into all Truth;	All history is interpreted by the provision of Jesus Christ.
Information mush: "How do we decide right from wrong?"	Norming	A universal standard of morality against which we judge our behavior	. . . will convict the world of sin, righteousness, and judgment;	All humanity is judged by the person of Jesus Christ
Information pollution: "How do we bring hope out of despair?"	Futuring	An exciting vision of the future in which we see our part.	. . . will show you things to come."	All hope is foreseen in the promise of Jesus Christ.

mind without emotion or will. To complete the chart and honor the third Person of the Trinity, the Christian world view must be internalized through spiritual experience which will enable us to live meaningfully, morally, and maximally in the coming Age of Information.

HOW DO WE EXPERIENCE
THE SPIRIT OF TRUTH?

In the Hi/Tech world, truth is a commodity. Parker Palmer in his book, *To Know As We Are Known/A Spirituality of Education*, analyzes the words which are the currency of education today: *fact, theory, objectivity* and *reality.* At their roots,

> *facts* mean "to manufacture" as a product;
> *theory* means "to view" as a spectator;
> *objective* means "to manipulate" for one's advantage; and
> *reality* means "to own" as a piece of property.[1]

In this context, truth is something "out there" to be made, observed, manipulated and owned. This is rationalism at its best — and at its worst. The sin of the Garden was the epistemological sin — pursuing knowledge for its own sake, assuming that this is the path of wisdom and finding it to be the way to sin and death. Physicists at Los Alamos pursued the "pure" research of splitting the atom, and then "applied" that knowledge to the invention of the atomic bomb. Robert Oppenheimer, the leader of the team, said, "We had to invent the bomb — it was so technologically sweet." But after he heard about the devastation of Hiroshima when that bomb was dropped, he then said, "The physicists have known sin."

In reaction against the extreme rationalism of high technology, Naisbitt says that people will swing to the other extreme, seeking truth in Hi/Touch human relationships; or, as Palmer says, "Projecting your psyche on the screen of the world." In the Hi/Touch search for truth, facts are paraded for feelings, objectivity for subjectivity, and reality for fantasy. Why is it that Silicon Valley, the Mecca of high technology, is also the place of erotic sex, exotic religions and ecstatic experience? Are cults and fantasies a Hi/Touch way in which we try to put the world together?

Without denying the value of reason and relationships as approaches to knowledge, Jesus informs us that only in the transcending truth of the Spirit's revelation can we put our world together.

How then does the Hi/Truth of the Spirit apply to our teaching/learning task? For years we have talked about the integration of faith and learning as a task to be accomplished within the concepts and by the disciplines of our intellectual tradition. More often than not we have failed. Is it possible that the integration of faith and learning is in our spiritual heritage, not in our intellectual tradition? As complementary reading for *Megatrends,* I recommend Parker Palmer's book. He may edge too close to the mystical for some of us, but I believe he brings us back to our roots in the recognition that "spirituality" is the missing ingredient in our intellectual quest as Christians. A recent survey of pastors brought out the confession that in the intensity of their theological studies and professional preparation, they fail to develop the spiritual disciplines and resources by which they can respond in depth to the needs of their people. Can we be equally honest? Our academic preparation may be sound, but does it prepare us with the spiritual resources required to respond to the "crisis of truth" in the Age of Information? We may try to make, observe, manipulate and own facts in the rational process, or express our feelings and our fantasies in the relational process, but still miss the truth because we have not experienced the Spirit of Truth in the revelational context.

Palmer also searches out the derivation of the word *truth.* It is a dramatic word meaning "troth" — not unlike the pledge of two lovers who give themselves to each other. Thus, to know the truth is to be betrothed to the Spirit of Truth. As Palmer says,

> . . . a relationship between the knower and the
> known — with which we are intimately bound in a
> relationship forged of trust and faith.[2]

After a third of a century in Christian education, I am now convinced that our future turns on the spirituality of our intellectual leaders. Without abandoning the rational or the relational, we must go beyond a personal commitment to Christ and a theological commitment to a statement of faith. A mutual commitment to spiritual development is even more important than professional development. Taking the lead, we must be pledged to the Spirit of Truth and be betrothed to spiritual disciplines by which the Spirit can lead us into all truth, convict us of sin, righteousness and judgment, and show us things to come. When we ask our students what they expect of Christian education and educators, they respond that they want to know us for our intellectual heights and our relational and caring reach, but perhaps more than anything else, they want to know our spiritual depths. To know the truth is to be engaged to the Spirit of Truth.

**MEGATRUTH, THEN, IS THE UNCHANGING WORD
OF GOD APPLIED TO THE CHANGING
CONTEMPORARY SCENE THROUGH
THE TEACHING OF THE SPIRIT OF TRUTH.**

PART III

MEGATRUTH FOR MEGATRENDS

New information and information-systems are affecting every aspect of the church, releasing for the first time its full potential to carry out The Great Commission.

10.
Hi/Touch for Our Relationships

At the close of a Sunday morning worship service, the pastor proposed, "Before you leave church this morning, tell five people that you love them, and in some cases, try a holy hug." His proposal reminds us that Christians are beginning to risk getting back in touch with their feelings — and with each other.

Not by coincidence and not without connection, American Telephone and Telegraph Company, one of the highest of Hi/Tech industries, spends millions of dollars on advertising to create a counter-image of human warmth, using the slogan: "Reach out and touch someone."

According to Naisbitt, there is a direct relationship between the rise of high technology and the return of Hi/Touch in human relationships.

THE HIGHER THE TECHNOLOGY,
THE GREATER OUR NEED FOR EACH OTHER.

In support of his premise, Naisbitt presents the evidence that spectacular advances in high technology during the 1960s were accompanied by a commensurate rise in such Hi/Touch movements as transactional analysis, human potential seminars, marriage encounter retreats and motivational workshops. The runaway best-seller, *I'm O.K., You're O.K.,* served as the popularized text for the process of self-discovery and the promise of self-esteem.

Evangelical Christians followed close behind. Keith Miller's book, *The Taste of New Wine,* introduced the era of relational theology based upon the premise that we will affirm in others what Christ affirms in us. Not to be outdone by secular self-searchers, evangelical Christians also flocked to workshops, seminars and retreats on self-esteem and interpersonal relationships. Robert Schuller rode on the high tide of the movement by borrowing on the image of Bishop Sheen and the idea of Norman Vincent Peale. His books and his television program reach both religious and secular audiences, and identify him as the most prominent personality of the relational era.

Along with the trend toward Hi/Touch in human relationships came the charismatic surge in religious experience. Its emphasis upon the "feeling" aspects of spiritual experience serves as a counterforce to the dehumanization of high technology and the desacrilization of the secular society. Not by coincidence, the charismatic movement arose in tandem with the advancements of high technology and the overload of information sources.

In their book, *The Year 2000,* Wiener and Kahn predicted that ecstatic religious experiences would become more prominent as society becomes more technological, bureaucratic and rational.[1] In fact, they foresaw the rise of religious cults as extreme reactions to the trauma of high technology. People who are highly educated, economically affluent, upwardly mobile and free from social restraints are particularly susceptible to cultic influences. Silicon Valley in California and similar Hi/Tech settings prove the prediction. Contrary as it may seem, the people who enjoy the benefits of high technology, and seem to have everything, are also the ones who lack authority over their own lives and warmth in their relationships. Perhaps the "Yuppies" — young, upwardly mobile professionals — whom we have too easily condemned — are really the pivotal population upon which a spiritual awakening in our generation depends. Contrary to our popular concept, spiritual awakenings are not generated in the masses and among the disenfranchised. It is the middle class, or its equivalent in a society, that has the economic, political and intellectual power to renew the culture, reform the society and raise the economic level of the poor. Without forsaking our commitment to the masses or our compassion for the poor, we must realize that the real contest for the minds, dollars, votes and souls is taking place at the middle level of social class. Here the battle is to be won or lost.

Cult involvement is an extreme that most of us will resist. In our need for Hi/Touch human relationships, we are more vulnerable to the wiles of self-interest in our spiritual experience. If best-sellers in Christian bookstores are any indicator, evangelical Christians have been preoccupied with the personal introspection and problems of interpersonal relationships since the 1960s. Naisbitt shakes us up when he reports that our response to satellite communication has not been to look outward upon a larger world, but to look inward at ourselves. When this happens, we lose the meaning of self-sacrifice. We cannot commit ourselves to a higher cause or give ourselves in service to others. A missions executive has already noted this change of attitude among missionary candidates. He said that they now ask for conditional commitments, short-term assignments, non-binding appointments and guaranteed security for their families. What a contrast with the oft-told story of the dying missionary who scrawled on the sand of the foreign shore, "No returns, no regrets, no reservations!"

Self-interest, with its inward look, will become a looming threat and a ready temptation as high technology takes over more and more aspects of our lives. It is a subtle sin of attitude that cannot be readily identified in human behavior. In fact, self-interest can be extolled as a virtue. A newspaper columnist recently wrote an editorial on the virtue of greed. Economic greed, he said, is the basis for the entrepreneurial motive which can prompt production and provide the base for raising the standard of living in a culture. To be sure, his argument represented classic capitalism, which is not without its flaws. But we cannot fault the power of his case when he cites example after example of communist and socialist nations returning to self-interest and free enterprise in their economic policy.

When Jesus reiterated the first and greatest commandment, "You shall love the Lord your God with all your heart, soul, mind and strength, and your neighbor as yourself," He gave value to self-interest and meaning to self-esteem. The danger is to make the drive for self-interest or self-esteem an end in itself. Daniel Yankelovich in his book, *New Rules: Living in a World Turned Upside Down,* finds that the generation of the 1970s, which pursued radical self-interest to its dead end in the 1980s, now wants the best of all worlds.[2] That generation wants the warmth and security of human commitment without giving up the freedom to pursue self-interest. This is impossible. No one can extend oneself without giving oneself. Otherwise, when commitment is put to the test, self-interest will overrule.

Conditional spiritual commitment which teeters on the rising and falling motives of self-interest is a major challenge to the church in the Age of Information. Self-interest can only pay lip service to biblical doctrine, give shallow pretense to spiritual discipline and selectively apply the Great Commission. If the time comes when it costs something to be a Christian in our nation, those whose faith is motivated by self-interest will be the first to fall out.

SELF-EXTENSION IS EVIDENCE
OF MATURE SELF-INTEREST.

A mature person is an individual who sacrifices self-interest for self-extension. Four qualities characterize self-extension in a mature person:

1. Immediate gratification is deferred for long-term goals;

2. visceral needs are subjected to the higher satisfaction of psychological, social and spiritual values;

3. attention is focused outwardly rather than inwardly; and

    4. concern is for others rather than for oneself.

Self-interest as an end in itself fails on all four counts. Immediate gratification, visceral fulfillment, persistent introspection and protective self-concern dominate the motives of an immature person. In the two most popular television programs of the mid-1980s, which communicate models for the American character, the profile is a person of self-interest. Whether it is a Carrington in "Dynasty" or a Ewing in "Dallas," it is a rare moment when a member of either family defers self- gratification for long-term goals, discipline for visceral desires, or extends beyond himself to any larger social responsibility. For the most part, persons are objects to be manipulated and used to achieve short, self-justifying ends.

Christians who presume that they can bathe themselves in the values of the secular media without contamination are playing games of self-deception. After a while, the blush is gone and the shock is dulled. We accept sin as lifestyle. Once having made that compromise, it is a short step to justifying the same sins in our own behavior.

My mother used to say, "The world is no friend to grace."

Today, we can also say, "The media is no aid to growth." If we look to the models of the media for our maturity, we will be stunted by the impediments of self-interest and selfish indulgence.

Self-extension is a value beyond the well-known hierarchy of needs proposed by Maslow. In ascending order, his scale rises from physiological needs through the needs of safety, belonging and esteem to self-actualization, which he considers the highest need.[3] It is notable that Maslow makes a distinction between self-esteem and self-actualization. Status and recognition are the major factors in self-esteem, whereas self-actualization is reaching one's potential as a person. Still, Maslow's definition of self-actualization falls short of self-extension because the value is still inwardly focused upon the natural self. A humanistic view of personality is the fault line in Maslow's theory. He assumes that a person can rise to self-actualization through the sequential fulfillment of lesser needs and through the fulfillment of the natural self. It should come as no surprise, then, to find his hierarchy of needs stopping short of self-extension, which requires sacrifice of the natural self.

Kohlberg's theory of moral development comes closer to the concept of self-extension as a quality of personal maturity. His research suggests three developmental levels in making moral judgments.[4] Level I is based upon self-interest, or pre-conventional judgment. Rewards and punishments are the positive and negative motivators for doing moral good. Level II is a step up to what Kohlberg calls "conventional judgment," in which the focus shifts to others. Interpersonal relationships, however, are still determined by rules and regulations. Level III identifies the highest order of moral good and post-conventional judgment, according to Kohlberg's scheme. Moral judgments are made according to principles that are intrinsically held by the individual. Neither fear nor rules determine the moral good for a person at this level. Right decisions are made because they are consistent with the internal principles to which the individual is committed.

SACRIFICIAL LOVE IS THE SELF-EXTENSIVE GOAL OF CHRISTIAN MATURITY.

While Maslow and Kohlberg contribute to our understanding of self-extension for personal and moral development, they still leave us grasping for the meaning of the term in a spiritual context. Peter, in his second Epistle, comes to our rescue with an inspired hierarchy of spiritual development. In ascending order, Peter envisions our spiritual growth as we build quality upon quality for Christian character:

faith,
virtue,
knowledge,
self-control,
fortitude,
piety,

> brotherly kindness
> love (2 Peter 1:5-7).

A full theory for spiritual development could be built on this scriptural model. For our purposes at this time, however, it is sufficient to note that self-giving love is the quality that characterizes the highest level of Christian maturity. We also note that it is built upon brotherly kindness, but distinct from it. Both qualities represent self-extension. The difference is the cost to the giver, not the recipient of the gift.

Brotherly kindness is an act of charity which is expected among friends and neighbors. Moments ago, a neighbor who heard about an accident which put my wife in bed called to ask if she could bring dinner in for us tonight. Then she added, "I am a member of the hospitality committee for the church. May we bring in meals next week?" This was an act of sisterly kindness that required sensitivity to our needs, care for us as neighbors, and a willingness to give the time, energy, and cost of a meal for us. In no way am I devaluing the gift of kindness to us. She was exhibiting the quality of a high level of spiritual maturity. Yet, each of us knows that our non-believing neighbor would do the same thing for us. Perhaps the motive springs from a humanitarian rather than a Christian impulse, but it would be difficult to establish the difference. Certainly, our spiritual development as Christians must lead us to act at least as loving as the best of pagans in response to the needs of our friends and neighbors. We know that the Word of God instructs us to care for those who are needy among us.

When the New Testament church held all its goods in common, the singular purpose was to meet the needs of all its members. Without doubt, the Body of Christ is a unique community of economic as well as spiritual interdependence. Furthermore, it is linked to the needs of Christians around the world through its missionary programs. When disaster strikes, whether by accident at home or famine abroad, Christians are quick to respond. Brotherly kindness has many dimensions, some of which are unique to the church, but most of which are better defined as humanitarian acts motivated by the relationship with those whom we call brother, sister, friend, or neighbor.

The love which Peter places at the highest level of Christian virtues is qualitatively different from brotherly kindness. It is the love given to us by Jesus Christ for our redemption — costing Him His life in order to save those who are His enemies. C. S. Lewis, in his inimitable way, helps us to understand the distinction between brotherly kindness and self-giving love in his book, *Four Loves,* when he writes,

> Divine gift-love . . . desires what is simply best for the beloved. . .

> Divine gift-love in a man enables him to love what is not naturally loveable: lepers, criminals, enemies, morons, the sulky, the superior, and the sneering.[5]

If spiritual maturity is measured by our demonstrations of self-giving love, most of us fall far short of the goal. We pride ourselves in our periodic displays of brotherly kindness, but avoid the places of risk and the kinds of people which put our Christlike love to the test.

WHAT'S GOOD FOR THE CHRISTIAN IS GOOD FOR THE CHURCH.

Churches are also personalities with qualities of character and potential for growth. As with individuals, institutions can be invaded by attitudes of self-interest which stunt their growth toward spiritual maturity. Jesus' commendations and condemnations of the seven churches of Asia in the Book of Revelation can be read accurately as a progress report on their spiritual development toward the maturity of self-giving love. Essentially, they were judged for the same qualities by which self-extension is defined.

Were they driven by *short* or *long-term* goals?

Were they giving priority to *material* or *spiritual* needs?

Were they focusing their attention *inwardly* or *outwardly?*

Were they concerned about *themselves* or *others?*

If today's churches were measured on these same standards, many would lose their candlesticks. While professing and publicizing a ministry of self-extension, a critical review of programs, practices, attitudes and aspirations would reveal the hidden priorities of short-term goals, materialistic ambitions, inward focus and ethnocentric concern. Certainly, the move toward relational theology and Hi/Touch ministries brings the church into contact with the flesh-and-blood issues of the real world. But with the relational emphasis comes the danger of turning inwardly toward perpetual self-interest and becoming stunted in growth toward self-giving love. Hi/Touch ministries can create dependencies that are self-reinforcing, as can any therapeutic program. The goal must be independent people with the strength of self-worth by which they can give themselves to others.

Jesus gives us an example of self-extension in the healing of the madman of Gadarenes. After being freed from demon-possession, the grateful man asked Jesus if he could stay with Him. The answer was, "Go home to thy friends, and tell them how great things the Lord hath done for thee, and hath had compassion on thee" (Mark 5:19). Jesus knew the dangers of dependency, especially in dealing with psychological problems and emotional needs. So he set the man free, sent him home, and instructed him to extend himself by witnessing to his friends.

SELF-EXTENSION CHARACTERIZES
A MATURE CHURCH
AS WELL AS A MATURE CHRISTIAN.

The challenge of self-extension applies to the church as well as to the individual. We know, for instance, that the tighter the bonds of interpersonal relationships in the church, whether ethnic, emotional, social or spiritual, the more resistant the church is to change and the less receptive it is to bringing new and different people into the fellowship. The satisfaction of sharing together can create a dependency cycle that feeds upon itself; the security of being together can limit the church to acts of brotherly kindness which cost little in either commitment or sacrifice.

KNOWLEDGE ABOUT
NEW AND CHANGING HUMAN NEEDS
WILL TEST THE MATURITY OF THE CHURCH
IN THE AGE OF INFORMATION.

From every sector of the nation and around the globe, we are being flooded with information about new and changing human needs. On the world scene, for example,

one billion people go to bed hungry each night;

500 million people are starving to death;

40,000 children are dying from hunger and disease each day.

At home, new information is even more startling because it contradicts our expectations:

60 percent of our marriages end in divorce;

single-parent families, usually a working mother and a child, represent the fastest-growing households in the nation;

children of single-parent families are the "new poor" among us, living below the poverty level, without adequate food, clothing, shelter or health care;

people aged sixty-five and older are the fastest-grow-ing segment of the nation's population;

Hispanics will be the largest ethnic minority in the nation by the end of the decade;

for the first time in our history the children of this generation are less well-off than their parents;

the gap between the rich and the poor, the "haves and the have-nots" among us, is increasing;

13 percent of our high school graduates are function-ally illiterate and 25-30 percent of our population are functionally "aliterate" — they can read, but do not; and

one out of twelve families in the United States is rocked by domestic violence.

From every sector in the nation and around the globe, we are being flooded with instant information about new and changing needs among different categories of people. One of two reactions is open to us. The natural tendency is to withdraw into the comfort of our own kind. The other is to develop a world awareness with a heightened sense of responsibility for the needs of others. As Christians, we will be held accountable for the information we receive. Again, we have the choice of self-interest or self-extension.

SELF-EXTENSION FOR THE CHURCH IN THE AGE OF INFORMATION MEANS SAVING AND SERVING THOSE WHO ARE NOT OF OUR OWN KIND.

The church of Jesus Christ is said to be the only social institution that exists primarily to serve those who are not its own. Somewhere in our pilgrimage we have either lost or forgotten this motive. If we think about the balance of the church today between serving its own and serving others, the scale tips heavily toward self-service. For the church in the Age of Information, however, the scale must tip again. In a convicting article in *Christianity Today,* James Earl Massey

writes about our responsibility to people who are different in
color, class or creed:

> It was John A. MacKay who first said in print
> that "the human symbol of our time is the outsider."
> That figure can serve to focus our work, which is
> reaching maturity with redemptive concern so that
> we make *insiders* with Christ and ourselves.[6]

In response to the challenge, we must begin with the *outsiders among us*. The facts are in and the projections are unavoidable. The composition of the church is changing. As noted, in the general population, the fastest-growing segment is people who are sixty-five years of age and older. Although all of our social institutions are being affected by the aging of America, Congress is slow to face the reality that Social Security can go bankrupt because there will not be enough wage-earners to support the retirees. We are equally slow to make the personal adjustments for financial planning, for medical care, and for living costs on an extended and inflationary actuarial table. Advertising, however, is already anticipating the future for an aging population. Watch the shift of age appeal in commercials for McDonald's. After catering to the kiddie crowd with birthday parties and playgrounds, the ads included elderly people doing the rhythmical "hand-slapping" routine along with babies, kids, moms and dads of every class and color.

The church, with its service motive, can take a lesson from advertising. Perhaps more than other social institutions, the ministry of the church will be affected by its aging congregation. Yet, we must admit that our programs are still geared to the "Pepsi generation." H. Newton Malony, in the same *Christianity Today* series about "Trends Facing the Church," provides us with a most creative, yet threatening picture of the paradoxes with which the local church must deal as its congregation changes and grows elderly:

> smaller Sunday schools — more education;
> fewer revivals — more conversions;

> fewer meetings — more activities;
> fewer visits — greater care.[7]

The assumption behind Malony's projections is that aging people are ready for activity, not withdrawal. They are ready for mature learning of the Word, sound reflection on spiritual issues, active involvement in service ministries, and quality care when they become chronically ill.

Changing the emphasis of the church's ministry from youth to the elderly will be traumatic. If past patterns hold true, we will hang on to our youth orientation until we are forced to respond to the numbers and needs of the elderly. Then, sometime in the 1990s, we will enter the field of ministry to the aged as if it has just been discovered. Churches that take the lead will be extolled as models, successful pastors in the field will write books, seminaries will scramble to offer courses, and of course, there will be an evangelical World Congress on the Aging. It will be too late for a whole generation of aging people who will feel like outsiders within the church. Now is the time to face the facts, confront the paradoxes, anticipate the emerging needs, and balance our ministries. Applied research needs to be done by our scholars in Christian colleges and seminaries, pilot programs need to be established in churches, conferences on the subject of ministering to the elderly must be organized, and attitudes of clergy and laity must be shifted toward a full, three-generational context of youth, middle-age, and elderly.

Another quality of self-extension for the mature, Hi/Touch church will be to minister to *outsiders around us.* As the Chairman for the Division of Research and Development for the Greater Bluegrass United Way in Kentucky, I have seen how our studies of new and emerging human service needs have sent shock waves through our community. For instance, by tracing trends between the census of 1970 and 1980, we have found that single-parent families are the fastest-growing household in our relatively stable and conservative area. If the trend continues at the same rate of increase throughout the remaining years of the decade, single-parent families will be the majority household in our community by 1990. Other studies show that, by the turn of the decade, more than 50 percent of all children in the United States will come from single-parent families.

The fallout from these trends will test the desire of the church to respond to hurting people who are outsiders around us. For the most part, single-parent families are the result of divorce. Churches have struggled to uphold their standards for divorce in relation to membership and leadership among both laity and clergy. When one evangelical denomination wanted to qualify church membership for divorced people, an urban pastor stood up to plead, "If you do this, you will take away my ministry to at least half of my congregation."

The church must make some decisions. Do we change our *de jure* position against divorce while retaining *de facto* attitudes against divorcees and their families? Our hearts reach out to persons who are deserted or betrayed, but we still tend to mold our attitudes and model our ministries around the nuclear family. As a bright, brilliant and beautiful, twice-divorced woman told me at family camp in California, "I need something more from the church than the — forgive me — 'meat market' of another singles group." Her comment invited me to probe for her deeper needs. She talked around the subject until a teenage girl ran by, skidded to a stop, and hugged her mother. Then the woman admitted, "She's starting to date, and I can't help her because I'm turned off on men. She needs a mature Christian man for a model. That's how the church could help me most right now."

Her words spoke volumes, because a Hi/Touch church professes to be the "family of God." The question is whether or not the church can be the self-extended family of God to meet the needs of the wounded who come to us for healing and help. The test is on.

Information about the personal, social and spiritual needs of single-parent families is now making ripples that will make waves in the 1990s. Single parents are usually women whose standard of living is radically reduced after divorce. Employment is required, but these parents usually can find only low-paying jobs because of the lack of professional skills. Day-care centers become substitutes for the home in training children during formative years. Later, "latch-key kids" shift for themselves after school, before mother comes home. The saddest fact, however, is the evidence that children of single-parent families are the "new poor" among us — living below the poverty level without adequate food or health care. A grim future awaits the children of single-parent families in the 1990s. If the church is to reach out and touch single parents and their children, we must begin by rethinking the biblical meaning of "the family of God," realigning our ministries in accord with their needs, and reworking our compassion for those who are outsiders among us.

Still another challenge for the Hi/Touch church in the Age of Information are the *outsiders who are beyond us*. The greater the diversity of people, the greater the distance we put between ourselves and them. Ethnic minorities, particularly those of a different color, culture and class serve as a disturbing example. James Earl Massey, in the *Christianity Today* article quoted earlier, pleads with us on behalf of his black people:

> While there is not a lot of encouragement in our society for unified, calculated, unrestricted ministry among people, it is nevertheless an action on the side of the future as God wills it. The social setting still poses, postures, and prefers; it cares all too little about how circumstances, history and preconditioning have blocked our togetherness in mind and spirit and life. *The shame is that the problems of distance in our society are also felt in the church.* [8]

More than two decades have passed since Congress passed civil rights legislation and the Supreme Court ruled against racial discrimination. Comparing the current situation with the past status of blacks, it appears as if they have made more gains in the secular society than they have in the church. With the lifting of social pressure and the shifting of civil rights issues toward other minorities, such as women and homosexuals, we have relaxed our efforts to bridge the distance between the "white" church and the "black" community. Does this mean that our theology of personal worth and our doctrine of social justice rise and fall under social pressure rather than being constantly and consistently honed by biblical truth?

Without having answered the question regarding black people, we were chilled by another cold blast of new information. *In the 1990s, Hispanics will be the largest ethnic minority in the nation.* Naisbitt's *Megatrends* includes the migration of our population to the South and Southwest. In both of these regions, Hispanics are multiplying in numbers and increasing in influence. Naisbitt also predicts that Florida may soon take over first position from California as the flagship state of the future. Why? Because Florida is the state of retirees and Hispanics. In Florida we see our future — a bigenerational, bicultural and bilingual nation.

Dr. Raymond Bakke, our leading evangelical urbanologist, tells a story that convicts us while we chuckle. A cat is chasing a mouse down an urban street. As the cat is about to catch its prey, the mouse falls into an open manhole and lands on a ledge just out of reach of the cat. The mouse cowers on the ledge as the claws of the cat swing just over its head. Suddenly, the paw is withdrawn as the mouse hears the angry sound of a barking dog. Relieved to know that the cat has been chased away, the mouse climbs out of the sewer only to be snatched by the cat. Just before death, the mouse manages the question, "But what happened to the dog?"

Gleefully, the cat answers, "Don't you know? If you want to survive in the city, you have to be bilingual."

While bilingual refers only to language, it represents the culture of outsiders who are beyond us. Whether blacks, Hispanics, Asians or Africans, James Massey's words speak the mandate for our ministry in the coming decade:

> Evangelicalism thrives only where there is a passion
> for people — and a historical consciousness about

their worth that is readily inclusive and biblically just.[9]

Thus, along the *Megatrend* toward a Hi/Tech-Hi/Touch society, we come to this *MegaTruth:*

THE HI/TOUCH CHURCH IN THE AGE OF INFORMATION MUST EXTEND ITS RELATIONAL REACH TO OUTSIDERS AND GIVE ITSELF TO BRING THEM IN.

11.
Hi/Test for Our Stewardship

If you want to start an argument among American Christians, introduce the subject of economics. As beneficiaries of capitalism, there is a tendency to equate prosperity with the favor of God and to elevate an economic system to a level just short of gospel truth. Our position is justified by the bankruptcy of the welfare state, the atheism of socialist ideology, and the Marxist mix of liberation theology. To suggest the redistribution of wealth in order to reduce the growing gap between the rich and the poor is to run the risk of condemnation as being un-American, if not un-Christian.

Economics is a subject that some of us remember as a dreaded requirement for high school graduation. At worst we hated it; at best we tolerated it. Perhaps we remember the law of supply and demand or the names Adam Smith and Lord Maynard Keynes in order to score points in Trivial Pursuit, but we have retained little else. Most certainly we did not see the moral and spiritual implications of economics for the future of the church.

Now we are paying a high price for our ignorance and our neglect. In the futuristic studies funded by The Rockefeller Foundation, economics, communications and public affairs are cited as the professions that will have greatest impact upon the quality of life in our society. Yet, by-and-large, these are the professions in which Christians have the least influence. Economics, in particular, is an evangelical wasteland. In preparation for writing this book, I scoured the profession for an evangelical Christian with stature in the field of economics. At that time, the closest I could come was the exchequer to the Queen of England.

Other symptoms of our economic ignorance are plentiful. Robert Dugan, Director of the Public Affairs Office of the National Association of Evangelicals in Washington, D.C., reports that senators and representatives in Congress are deluged with letters from evangelical Christians on such issues as prayer in public schools, pornography, and equal time for religious broadcasting. Letters expressing concern about our escalating national deficit, however, are almost non-existent. This lack of economic understanding is reinforced by Jerry Falwell's decision to change the name of the Moral Majority to the Liberty Federation. His avowed intent is to address political issues that are not moral, such as the federal budget.

To the contrary, the spiraling deficit may crash under the weight of moral concerns. President Reagan himself used an analogy to illustrate the magnitude of the issue. He said that $1 million is equal to a four-inch stack of 1000-dollar bills. In comparison, the federal budget is a stack of 1000-dollar bills rising 367 miles into the air! To date, the impact of that deficit upon our national economy and personal standard of living is minimal because we are following the philosophy of "Spend now, pay later." In the long-term, however, we are mortgaging the future of our children. They will be the ones to pay higher taxes with reduced benefits and suffer the drop in their standard of living. To say that the federal budget is not a moral issue is to reveal short-term political thinking rather than long-term economic responsibility. If the current trends continue, our economic future will have this profile:

> Non-productive military spending will absorb a higher share of the federal budget;

social programs to meet human service needs, such
as those of the poor, hungry, elderly, handicapped
and sick will be further reduced;

the widening gap between the rich and the poor will
become a chasm filled with hatred;

the standard of living for each generation will be
lower than that of the preceding generation; and

severe conflict will arise between the minority of
younger wage earners and the majority of elderly
voters on such issues as Social Security and
Medicaid.

Many other facts can be marshaled to show the long-term
moral implications of a runaway federal deficit and our short-
term moral responsibility for federal budgeting. The conclusion
is unavoidable.

CHRISTIANS ARE PAYING A HIGH PRICE FOR ECONOMIC IGNORANCE AND NEGLECT.

Self-interest rears its ugly head again. If we are content
with our economic position in life, we will protect that position
by embracing the status quo and avoiding the larger, long-term
issues of our social responsibility. Economic self-interest can
even twist our motives for ministry. Jesus had scalding words
for the scribes who "devoured widows' houses" by pretending
to serve them as financial counselors while harboring the mali-
cious motive of gaining control over their assets. Some current
and prosperous Christian ministries are subject to a similar
accusation. Because economic integrity is foundational to the
effectiveness of our Christian witness in the secular world, a
group of concerned leaders in parachurch ministries organized
the Evangelical Council for Financial Accountability. Biblical
principles for economic integrity and professional standards for
fiscal responsibility were established as the criteria for membership. To carry the logo of the EFCA on official publications

gives fiscal credibility in both the Christian and secular communities. Regrettably, some of the most prominent and prosperous ministries refuse to meet the standards of accountability.

Still, evil intent is not our major economic problem. It is
economic ignorance and neglect that makes us vulnerable to
secular economic attitudes by default. For instance, we may
carry over our *consumer mentality* into our religious choices.
The voracious appetites that we seek to satisfy by conspicuous
consumption may dictate the church we attend, the theology
we believe, the spiritual experience we accept, and the lifestyle
we pursue. Especially for mobile people in an urban setting,
churches can become a spiritual smorgasbord from which people
choose foods for color, taste, and satisfaction more than for
nutritional value and a balanced diet. Denominational loyalty
and even biblical integrity can give way to social compatability
and spiritual comfort. It is just a step, then, to the personalistic
and privatistic religion which Martin Marty describes as the
faith of the "high-rise apartment and the long weekend."[1] As
consumers of religion, we can pick and choose among churches,
substitute small groups for corporate worship, go to church by
television or hold our faith in private. The carry-over of our
consumer mentality may well be a greater threat for the future
of the church than secularism itself.

Close behind our consumer mentality is the *prosperity
syndrome.* Some television evangelists lead the way with promises of success and prosperity as a reward for Christian faith.
Not by coincidence, three television preachers at the same time
were giving away books on financial planning for Christians.
Their motives must surely be mixed. While performing a needed
service for Christians, they seem also to be building a base
for gifts to their ministries.

The theology behind the prosperity syndrome is even more
suspect. Historically, it ties into the much-maligned Puritan
ethic that supposedly linked hard work with success and prosperity as evidence of God's favor. The truth is that the idea is
more closely related to American cultural Christianity than to

biblical theology. Yet, in a time of affluence, it is a comforting argument.

Even our evangelism has been influenced by economics. The church growth movement has roots in *market theory* as well as in anthropology and missiology. Its identification of cultures which are most ready to respond to the gospel has the familiar ring of "affinity groups" in marketing theory. Its call for efficiency in targeting certain peoples for evangelism sounds like the strategic planning of a marketing group. Its concept of "contextualization" which weaves the presentation of the gospel into the cultural setting is not unlike the "exchange of values" which is the primary principle of marketing theory. Effective evangelism as demonstrated by Jesus and the apostles capitalized on marketing concepts, but they were not limited by the need for guaranteed success. There is wisdom in James Earl Massey's warning about marketing the church "lest an intended good backfire as a selfish search *for one's own kind.*"[2]

Extending the influence of economics upon our evangelical behavior one more step, we tend to follow the *capitalistic motive* in our giving. Socialism is based upon the premise that the state must provide directly for the human service needs of its people. The welfare state epitomizes socialism at its best — and worst. In contrast, capitalism assumes that economic growth will benefit all of the people as the standard of living is raised and private philanthropy responds to the needs of the poor, hungry, sick, handicapped and disadvantaged. In popular terms, capitalism counts on economic growth to raise the standard of living for all people, on government programs to provide a "safety net" for those who are helpless, and on private philanthropy to "trickle down" its benefits to the needy. Current evidence shows that the theory is better than the practice. Our economy is rising and yet our standard of living is falling; our safety net of government programs has gaping holes through which the poor, hungry, sick and elderly are falling; and our philanthropy is often guided by "identifiable self-interest" rather than genuine human need.

Our personal giving also tends to be dictated by a capitalistic motive. Although tithing is a biblical principle, Christians give only three percent of their total income to the church and its related ministries. More than that, tithes are treated like discretionary income which can be given to sporadic appeals rather than sustaining ministries. Notably, while multiple millions of dollars were being given to Ethiopian famine relief, the budgets of ongoing ministries suffered serious losses. Worse yet, many Christians assume that their gifts to the work of the Lord come from "trickle down" dollars that are left over after basic needs and conspicuous wants are funded. In this sense, we are capitalists in theory, but not in practice.

CAPITALISM IS THE WORST SYSTEM OF ECONOMICS, UNTIL YOU CONSIDER THE ALTERNATIVES.

Make no mistake, I am an advocate and a beneficiary of capitalism. Economic free enterprise is a companion to democracy and fits the quip made by Winston Churchill when he said, "Democracy is the worst possible system of government . . . until you consider the alternatives." If for no other reason than for being the climate of freedom within which the church can flourish, capitalism is worthy of our support as Christians. The right of human freedom is a biblical standard against which governments must be measured. But we must never forget that capitalism and democracy are human systems that are capable of corruption and open to excesses. Once again, we appeal to the Spirit of Truth to teach us discernment. As we come out of the time of parenthesis into the Age of Information, economic attitudes and values will pose a crucial test for our biblical faith, with the potential of becoming a destructive wedge between believers, a protective hedge against the poor, or an unprecedented opportunity to demonstrate our compassion in the cause of social justice. Now is the time to face the economic realities posed by Naisbitt and defined as a megashift "From a National Economy to a World Economy." Naisbitt sums up the shift with two indisputable facts:

First, we are shifting from being an isolated, virtually self-sufficient national economy to being part of an interdependent global economy.

Second, we are giving up our former role as the world's dominant force and becoming a member of a growing handful of economically strong countries. [3]

Behind these facts is the impact of new information. Instant communication, of course, is changing all of the dimensions of world finance and creating a network of financial interdependence from which no nation is exempt. Consequently, we are having to rethink our economics at home and abroad. At home, for instance, facts about our spiraling federal deficit are matched by our declining balance in world trade. The plight of our farmers illustrates the interlocking relationship between our national and our global economy. When the grain sales with Russia were approved, American farmers went deeply into debt for new machinery, expecting that inflation would continue so that they could pay off their obligations with cheaper dollars. Just the opposite has happened. A worldwide collapse of commodity prices has been aggravated by a strong U.S. dollar in the global market because of interest rates on the federal deficit. At the end of the cycle is the American farmer who cannot compete with the lower prices of other nations for exported grain.

Another example of our economic global interdependence based upon new information is the "American" automobile. While our chauvinism causes us to put bumper stickers on the backs of our automobiles which read, "Made in America," the fact is that an all-American car is a thing of the past. In Pennsylvania, for instance, a city council passed an ordinance requiring that all official vehicles be exclusively American-made. After a thorough investigation of auto-makers the report came back that the only available all-American car was a Volkswagen!

Corporations are adjusting to this new economic reality by planning for global manufacturing and markets. In a strange pattern, American and foreign manufacturers are passing each other on the way to build plants overseas. Toyota, for example, has just announced that it will build an $800 million auto plant in our Bluegrass area. The impact upon the community is immediately significant. A research center on robotics has been planned for the University of Kentucky, a Japanese bank plans to open a new office in Lexington, and a local college has a waiting list for business executives who want to learn the Japanese language and system. On the other side of the ledger are tragic stories of community decay which follow the decision of a corporation to move its operation overseas. Especially where a "company town" is involved, people are trapped in the unemployment cycle, with no opportunity to move or be retrained. Contagious despair infects the whole city and the pall of economic death smothers any hope for the future. One can foresee laws which require that corporations make reparation for the economic devastation they leave behind when they close a plant or move overseas. Once again, the moral implications of economic decisions cannot be avoided.

More positively, corporations are teaching us the meaning of a global economy. Seeing the trends and anticipating the future, corporations are moving the focus for their business from the Northern to the Southern Hemisphere. Rather than limiting their headquarters to a single nation in the North, they are developing a triad of general offices in the United States, Western Europe and Japan in order to serve their southern counterparts in South America, Africa and Asia. Leadership must follow. In a book by Neil Chesanow entitled, *The World Class Executive,* the author foresees cross-cultural understanding as the key to successful corporate leadership in the future.[4] A global economy requires a global outlook.

ECONOMICS MAY WELL BE THE MOST SIGNIFICANT SOCIAL ISSUE FOR THE CHURCH IN THE AGE OF INFORMATION.

America is in its third century as a nation. In each of the first two centuries, historians see pivotal issues upon which the future of the nation turned and in which the church was involved. The War of Independence in the eighteenth century represented the struggle for freedom from the oppressive rule of England and political equality for every citizen. Out of the Great Awakening of the 1740s came the impulse for political freedom as a natural result of spiritual freedom. One hundred years later, the Civil War represented the drive for personal freedom for slaves and social equality for the black minority. Again, the impulse for the Abolitionist movement came from another Great Awakening earlier in the century. Christians led the way in a social revolution.

The question now confronting us is: What will be the social and moral issue of the twentieth century upon which the future of our nation turns? Is it

> morality in the media?
> pro-life rulings?
> nuclear disarmament?
> economic equality for the poor?

We are tiptoeing in another minefield. If, as we said earlier, our nation experienced a genuine spiritual awakening in the 1970s, then we can expect that prophetic voices will rise in the 1980s calling the church to some critical point of social responsibility which can reform the nation and leave the moral mark of the church upon our century.

Each of these issues is pivotal and of Christian concern. Economic equality for the poor, however, has a direct connection with the issues of the past that give it saliency. As with political and social equality, the heart of the issue of economic equality is *justice*. By and large, conservative Christians have been weak on this phase of our biblical responsibility. For some reason, in the split of the church between liberal and conservative factions, the concerns for social justice tended to go with the liberals while conservatives continued to be identified with acts of personal mercy. For example, in response to the problems of world hunger, liberals are in the forefront of action to get at the social and structural injustices which cause hunger, while conservatives lead in organizations such as World Vision, World Relief, Food for the Hungry and World Concern, which are primarily dedicated to relief and self-help programs.

In the Age of Information, both liberals and conservatives will be called to Micah's mandate for the affluent people of his nation:

> What doth the LORD require of thee, but to do justly, and to love mercy, and to walk humbly with thy God? (Micah 6:8)

Justice is to be done, mercy is to be given, and humility is to be shown by people whom God has prospered and sensitized to the needs of the poor. Not only on the national level, but also on the global level of our economy, must Christians deal with these moral dilemmas:

> What are the social costs of continuous economic growth?

> What are our priorities in a time of economic decline?

> How do we distribute wealth to reverse the widening gap between "haves" and "have nots?"

> How do we control the distribution of limited resources in an economic system based upon competition rather than cooperation?

Once again, these large economic questions converge with life-changing impact upon the individual. In the Age of Information, Naisbitt informs us, traditional work roles of skilled labor in the Industrial Age will give way to intellectual and service tasks. Unemployment will continue to create pockets of poverty and people of despair. Retraining of workers will be common; it is predicted that the average person will go through three or four retraining cycles in a lifetime. But the most severe disjuncture will be felt by persons who are "underemployed"

— educated for a profession or a skill that is overcrowded or obsolete. Studs Terkel, in his book, *Working,* concludes from his itinerant interviews across the nation, "Most of us . . . have jobs that are too small for our spirits."[5]

As the fall-out from the economic transition to the Age of Information, the church will have to include in its sphere of pastoral care the displaced, distressed and disillusioned persons whose sense of self-worth and meaning in life has been severly damaged by changing work roles.

BIBLICAL STEWARDSHIP IS HI/TEST
FOR THE CHURCH IN THE AGE OF INFORMATION.

In the fields of human knowledge, the church has found both friend and foe in the physical, biological and behavioral sciences. Especially in psychology, the findings of the field have been made "user friendly" with the church in its Hi/Touch emphasis. Economics, however, has remained an outsider except in the ideas and benefits that we have sanctified. Now, economics is coming forward as the behavioral science of the future, based on instant information which seals our global interdependence. The subject must be high on the agenda of the Hi/Truth church of the future. As a starter, the agenda must include:

> opening the debate over economic issues, such as the Roman Catholic bishops have done with their pastoral letters;

> developing a theology of stewardship that is biblically and economically sound;

> making the integration of faith and learning in economics a priority for Christian scholarship;

> requiring economics as a subject in Christian education from elementary to college levels;

> identifying economics as a field of study in which Christians should participate as "missionaries without portfolio";

separating Christianity from capitalism in our definition of orthodoxy;

extending our evangelical outlook to understand our
interdependence in the global economy, and relating
our world mission to the larger scene;

calling our political leaders to accountability for the
long-term, moral implications of our economic policy; and

taking positions of economic policy that give priority
to the causes of social justice for the poor, hungry
and sick both at home and abroad.

Macro-economics of a national and global economy, however, must be preceded by the micro-economics which are
immediately under our control. The church, as an institution,
must resist its tendency toward conspicious consumption in
personnel, program and plant. The Christian, as an individual,
must discipline the temptation to indulge in the kind of con-
sumerism that is motivated by self-interest and counterproductive
to efforts that call the church and our nation to economic
responsibility.

John Wesley is remembered for his visonary declaration,
"The world is my parish." In the Age of Information, his vision
will become our responsibility. As Marshall McLuhan reminded
us, "On Spaceship Earth, there are no passengers. We are all
crew."

**FOR THE WORLD PARISH
CREATED BY A GLOBAL ECONOMY,
WE ARE ALL MEMBERS OF THE CONGREGATION
AND STEWARDS OF ITS TRUST.**

12.
Hi/Energy for Our Organizations

On a cross-country trip with four children, our two-year-old blazed a trail from town to town with his shouts, "Mac — DON — ohs!" every time the Golden Arches came into view. No one will dispute the fact that McDonald's is one of the most successful franchising and marketing ventures of modern times. What does McDonald's have to do with shaping the church in the Age of Information? We shall see.

Four of the megatrends reported by Naisbitt bear directly upon the nature of our formal organizations. One is the megashift from *centralization to decentralization* in the direction of our organizations. Second is the movement from *institutional help to self-help* in the function of our institutions. Third is the change from *representative to participatory democracy* in the governing of our structures. Fourth is the transposition from *hierarchies to networks* — a fundamental change in the nature of our organizations. While each of these megashifts deserves discussion in detail, the trend from centralized to decentralized structures is the prime mover behind the other changes.

INFORMATION IS TURNING
ORGANIZATIONAL DEVELOPMENT
UPSIDE DOWN AND INSIDE OUT.

Institutions are originally formed to meet common needs
and achieve common goals. To be effective, an institution must
have leadership that interprets new information related to those
needs and goals in a continuing vision of institutional mission.
To be efficient, an organization must have leadership that
allocates available resources to meet those needs and achieve
those goals.

Sad to say, most institutions go through a process that
causes them to lose their primary purpose. Stage I is *agitation* —
people who find that their needs are not being met or their
goals achieved in existing institutions will come together to
form an organization. Stage II is *accommodation* — as the
agitation diminishes and the organization grows, attention is
shifted toward institutional stability and cultural credibility.
Stage III is *administration* — priority is given to preserving the
system rather than serving the people. When this happens, the
leadership of a bureaucracy retains its power by privileged
information and partisan distribution of resources. All of the
evils of a centralized system follow.

Churches are not exempt from the tendencies toward centralization. When I was a boy, a storefront mission was formed in
our community by members of a well-established church who
felt their spiritual needs were not being met. In their early
days, these church members had been vigorous evangelists on
our streets and noisy participants in their worship. Migrants
from the South who came North looking for work found a welcome home in the new fellowship, so the congregation soon
outgrew its meager sanctuary and moved to temporary quarters
in a local school. Within a few years, a church was built on
the fringe between the city and the suburbs. The congregation
began to grow and change. No longer did the pastor boycott
the local ministerial association, nor were the young women
required to wear their hair in a bun. Size dictated another
move, this time to the suburbs on a spacious site that could

accommodate their dreams for a recreation center, a day school and a retirement home, as well as a sanctuary seating 2500 people. At last report, a visitor to their services noted that neither the tone of the worship nor the class of the congregation could be distinguished from the church across town from which they had split. In the short span of 25 years, they had moved full cycle from agitation, through accommodation, to administration, in the process of centralization.

Information in the hands of the people is the key to reversing the direction from centralization to decentralization in institutional development. According to Naisbitt, decentralized farms represented the institutions of the Age of Agriculture. No mystery surrounds the reason for this pattern. Farming is a function which requires space and available resources, such as fresh water and fertile soil. With the coming of the Age of Industry, however, the direction of growth and productivity turned toward centralization. Industry requires massive resources at a center point for control, such as water, coal, gas, oil or steel, in order to be efficient. The Age of Information reverses the direction once again. Information is the lightest of industries, produced without waste, accumulated without bulk, and disseminated without wait. Therefore, if information is our new wealth and power, its focus is outward toward decentralized units. In short, the information industry is decentralized by nature.

Naisbitt's fundamental thesis that decentralization is the natural American condition may be faulty. Certainly, there is a case to be made for the drive toward decentralization in a democracy. Human nature, however, has a twin thrust toward security and freedom. When we are secure, we want our freedom, and when we are free, we seek security. Like the drunk man getting up on one side of the horse only to fall off on the other side, we tend to go from extreme to extreme. For instance, after the strong centralizing movement toward a welfare state in the 1960s and 1970s, we have seen the failure of the federal government to effect constructive change through national policy and federal dollars. The result has been a reaction toward individual rights that is driven by self-interest. Even now, some social analysts fear what George Cabot Lodge has called "a totalitarian lurch" in reaction to the excesses of individual rights.[1] More accurately, democracy is a finely-tuned balance between our social responsibility and our personal freedom.

The same might be said for the countering forces of centralization and decentralization in organizations. Taken to their extremes, centralization leads to authoritarianism and decentralization ends up in anarchy. In *Megatrends,* Naisbitt misses the balance between these movements by assuming that decentralization is the natural condition of our democracy. He writes,

> Centralized structures are crumbling all across America. But our society is not falling apart. Far from it. The people of this country are rebuilding America from the bottom up into a stronger, more balanced, more diverse society.[2]

Naisbitt cites strong evidence for this generalization — primarily the megashift of political power from the federal government to the regions, states and especially the local level. To the extent that the federal government has failed to develop national policy governing the health, education and welfare of our people, I agree with him. The diversity of our land and the differences in our people do not lend themselves to national policies which presume that the federal government has superior knowledge of what the people in Peoria need. Yet, in tracing the trend toward decentralization, Naisbitt does not distinguish the role of the federal government in international policy or in national affairs which involve the destiny of all our people. Creative federalism is not antithetical to state's rights or local initiative.

Still, we must recognize the fact that new information in the hands of the people is bringing power to the point of function at the local level of government. Naisbitt notes that decentralization means:

> more centers of power;
> more opportunities for involvement;
> more choices for individuals;

more sensitivity to problems;
more power to create change.

All of this at a lower cost!

WHAT ARE THE IMPLICATIONS OF THE DECENTRALIZING INFLUENCE OF INFORMATION FOR THE ORGANIZATION OF THE CHURCH?

As with other social institutions, the church will be reshaped inside-out and from the bottom up in the Age of Information. The local church will be the center of action and the lay congregation will be the locus of power. Along with these decentralizing shifts will come greater diversity and specialization in the ministry of the church.

Information is power in the hands of the people of the church as well as in the society at large. Centralized power in a denomination, parachurch organization or independent ministry is created and maintained by privileged information in the hands of leaders who interpret that information for the people. In its extreme form, privileged information sustains dictatorships through the use of propaganda, which is nothing more than a one-sided interpretation of information by a centralized authority. Studies of propaganda indicated that dictators must not permit bits of counter-information to enter their communication system or they risk creating rebellion among the people. Ironically, Communist Russia has a single, state-controlled newspaper called *Pravda,* the Russian word for "truth." Because the newspaper interprets all of the news according to the Communist Party line, it contains no detracting advertising or dissenting columns. At its best, *Pravda* is a bore.

As a boy, I attended an independent church that was organized around a pastor who dominated the minds of the people. His word had the authority of the Word of God and his sermons dictated the lives of the people. Occasionally, dissenters would contest his authority, but with the pulpit as the point of control, they invariably lost and had to leave the church. Finally, the people got information about a problem that involved the pastor's integrity as well as his authority. The evidence was indisputable and the church eventually dissolved. Privileged information tends toward centralization, and open information tends toward decentralization.

Church leaders, whether bishops, presidents, or superintendents, depend upon privileged information to exercise their authority and maintain their position. The Roman Catholic Church is the prime example. Power in the Roman Catholic Church is top-down with the Pope speaking *ex cathedra* on matters of faith and morals. His word is infallible. The tension in the Roman Catholic Church today is information-related. Rising opposition to the position of the Pope on birth control, for instance, builds out of information about population growth in undeveloped nations that cannot feed, clothe, educate or employ the masses and from information about the prohibitive cost of maintaining the standard of living for large families in the western world.

Protestants broke the infallible authority of the Pope on matters of information, but retained the tendency toward centralized organization by giving top leadership the power of privileged information. One look at mainline denominations shows hierarchies and bureaucracies on a paralyzing scale. Smaller denominations, parachurch organizations and independent ministries are not exempt. Even though they may have begun as a grassroots reaction against a rigid hierarchy or bureaucracy that lost touch with the needs of the people, they too are subject to the seductive influence toward centralization.

Decentralization is making the local church the center of action. Although we have given lip service to this reality for years, the fact is that the local church is still a threat to centralized authority. Top leadership is still trying to create structures, ranging from organic union to federated fellowships that are presumed to represent the creative thrust of the church. Hierarachies still presume to control the policies of the church even though the laity are calling different signals. The most obvious conflict comes in mainline denominations with declining membership. While top leaders are devoted to unions, councils, and federations as the wave of the future, the laity are calling for spiritual renewal, doctrinal purity, evangelistic ministries, and world missions as the hope for the church. Three choices confront the laity who live with this dilemma. They may leave the church, as millions have done in recent years. They may opt for spiritual identity with independent ministries, privatized religion, or the electronic church. Or they may build their loyalty to the local church as the hope for spiritual renewal, the center of action and the place of change. In the latter case, the tension will continue to mount between the leadership of denominations and local congregations. Even now, we sense the reluctance of local congregations to send their budgetary apportionment to central headquarters because they do not agree with the direction of top leaders, do not see the spiritual results of their investment in denominational programs, or do not believe that they are receiving benefits for the ministry of the local church commensurate with their contribution. To avoid damaging splits between the central organization and local churches, our question is: How can we reshape the organization of the church to utilize the strengths of centralized authority and localized ministries?

Diversification is a companion to decentralization. The more information that is placed in the hands of the people, the greater the diversity of persons. Not many years ago, the local congregation served as a melting pot for individual differences. To be Christian meant commonalities, not only of belief and experience, but also of moral outlook and life style. Now, however, like American society in general, information about our differences has made us alphabet soup — cooking in the same broth, but retaining the individuality of our *A*'s through *Z*'s. Today, in the same congregation, there can be members who are:

> charismatics and non-charismatics;
> pro-lifers and pro-choicers;
> wine drinkers and teetotalers;
> hawks and doves;
> simple life-stylists and Yuppies;

> evangelicals and fundamentalists;
> inerrantists and plenarists;
> blacks and bilinguals;
> divorcees and single parents;
> preschoolers and senior citizens.

Of course, there has always been diversity of people in the church. The difference, today, is that we are aware of our individuality through information sources. In a sense, the local congregation is a tinder box of religious, moral and social differences that could be ignited at any time. If information creates diversity, we can count upon greater variation in the days ahead. Our question is: How can we maintain unity as diversity increases in the Body of Christ?

Specialization also comes with decentralizing and diversifying in the local congregation. For a relatively homogeneous congregation, the ministry of the church can be generalized to meet the needs of the people. I remember a church pattern that included common services for worship and prayer meetings, with complementary programs in graded Sunday school classes, a youth group and a women's missionary society. Recognition of the diversity of needs in today's congregation renders that pattern obsolete. Recently, I heard two pastors talking about the inadequacy of an age-graded Sunday school series for the specialized needs of people in their churches. "We need classes for divorcees, single parents, families with teenagers, college students and retirees. We need classes taught on subjects such as personal evangelism, media morality, political responsibility, cross-cultural communication, spiritual formation and Christian discipline."

The pastoral ministry itself is becoming more specialized. In large churches, the ministerial staff is expanding into professional roles for serving singles, ethnics, inner-city dwellers and senior citizens. Of course, in small churches the pastor must still be a generalist with the versatility to respond to specialized needs. The common denominator for all pastors, however, is the requirement for continuing education in order to stay abreast of the specialized skills required for ministering to greater diversity in local congregations. Our question is: How can we minister effectively to the specialized needs of our diverse congregations?

THE McDONALD'S MODEL OF THE CHURCH

In the book, *Corporate Cultures,* by Terrence E. Deal and Allan A. Kennedy, the organization of the future will consist of:

> small, task-oriented work units;
>
> each with economic and managerial control over its own destiny;
>
> interconnected with larger entities through benign computer and communication links;
>
> and bonded into larger companies through strong cultural bonds.[3]

The authors call this structure for the future an "atomized organization." It is small; its basic units are flexible because of its information resources; and it is bonded together into a strong, corporate whole through "shared cultural ties that define what the future of the company is all about."

Among the illustrations of corporations that are already organized for the future, the authors single out McDonald's — the most successful of the fast-food franchises. The genius of McDonald's is a high-energy balance between centralized resources and local services. Organizational structure, however, is not the key to its success. McDonald's strength is a strong culture of shared values that bonds all of the local franchises together. The standards of that culture are simple, clear and manageable — Quality, Service, Convenience and Value (QSCV). To assure that these standards are implemented in each local franchise, every McDonald's manager is trained at Hamburger University. The curriculum of the "University" is value-centered. Whatever the course — food preparation, employee relations, fast-food marketing or franchise management

— the singular goal is to prepare managers whose local leadership will personify Quality, Service, Convenience and Value at the local level.

The education of McDonald's managers is reminiscent of the preparation that Rome gave to its centurions who were to be assigned to commands in the far-flung provinces of the empire. In the book, *In Search of Excellence,* authors Robert H. Waterman, Jr., and Thomas J. Peters contend that the Roman Empire grew large and survived long because of the confidence that the emperor put in his centurions. After the best candidates for the role had been selected, they were thoroughly trained in the values of Rome — SPQR — Senatus Populusque Romanus, the Senate and the People of Rome. Then, when the centurians were assigned to the provinces, and their chariots disappeared through the gates of the city, there remained no doubt about their loyalty to Rome and their ability to establish the values of the empire in a distant land.[4]

McDonald's also provides continuing support for its standards. The common symbol of the Golden Arches is the assurance of Quality, Service, Convenience and Value. Advertising (with budgets that compete for first place in expenditures with beer and automobile commercials), constantly plays on the theme of the culture. A study of McDonald's television commercials is a full course in effective communication. One commercial, for instance, emphasizes the value of "convenience." A family is traveling across a remote part of the country. Someone wishes for a McDonald's hamburger. But the response is that there would be no McDonald's along the freeway of this desolate region. Surprise! Someone else looks up and sees the familiar sign just ahead. Convenience. Another ad features McDonald's new offering: biscuits for breakfast, with meat, cheese, and egg — under one dollar! Value. All of this advertising comes from corporate headquarters where the creative abilities of experts in television marketing are utilized to serve the local franchises.

Corporate headquarters also supports its local units by extolling the heroes of the system from its founder, Ray Kroc, to its Waitress of the Week. Unabashedly, McDonald's conducts contests and holds ceremonies throughout the system to create bonds between the corporate office and the local franchise.

One more critical function is reserved for the corporation through its regional supervisors who are constantly in the field. Quality control, morale building, trouble shooting and problem solving are their tasks. Periodic audits keep the local franchises accountable for the values of the McDonald's culture. One former McDonald's manager told me about "secret shoppers" who represent the regional office. Unbeknown to the manager or the clerks, they appear as customers to test the system.

Just recently, on my way to give a speech at a college, I stopped for coffee at a McDonald's restaurant along the freeway. As I drove up, I saw a banner hanging across the front announcing "Family Night — 29-cent hamburgers!!!" Who can pass up such a bargain? Inside the restaurant I stood out as a visitor in a business suit towering over a noisy gang of giggling pre-teen girls. When my turn came, the manager came over to the register, greeted me, speeded my order along, and left me with the comment, "Where else can you find a better value?"

Ah, ha, I thought, *he has mistaken me for a secret shopper.*

But when my suspicions subsided, I realized that he simply had reinforced the reason I stopped at McDonald's in the first place. Quality, Convenience, Service and Value.

With a strong culture built around shared values and supportive resources from corporate headquarters, local franchises of McDonald's are set free to determine their own managerial and economic destiny as small, task-oriented work units.

As a grandfather who is frequently commandeered as chauffeur for a trip to "Mac — DON — ohs," I do my own personal audit of the restaurant while monitoring the playground. The results are amazing. McDonald's could be a boring place because of the sameness of its architecture, decor, food and service. But something is different. One does not sit for long before a uniformed employee comes through the aisles sweeping up leftover hamburger papers, straws, napkins and kiddie food. I find myself conscientiously disposing of my tray and frowning at anyone who does not wipe the excess ketchup or milk shake off the table before leaving. The manager, who especially draws the attention of my critical eye, invariably demonstrates the principle of MBWA — Management By Walking Around. He or she not only keeps the system moving, but also steps into trouble spots to assure the quality and convenience of the service. And the manager sets the tone for the serving line. Although the "Welcome to McDonald's" varies in cheerfulness among the waiters or waitresses, I have yet to find a discourteous or impatient server. Every local franchise verbally and nonverbally communicates Quality, Convenience, Service and Value.

McDonald's gives us a model for the church of the future. Even though the process of decentralization makes the local church the center of action, there is still the need for a centralized resource unit that promotes a strong culture and provides a communication link among the churches. Imagine the reshaping of the church along the lines of the McDonald's model.

THE CORPORATE CHURCH — CENTER FOR RESOURCES

The corporate church complements the ministry of the local church as the center for leadership and service resources. Its functions are:

> to articulate the strategic vision for the church-at-large through its leadership;

> to communicate the culture of the church based upon shared values which define its past, present and future mission;

> to educate the clerical and lay leadership of the church in the vision and values of the culture through its educational institutions, including continuing education; and

to provide the information systems for assessing the
trends within the church-at-large and assisting the
local church in evaluating the effectiveness of its
ministries.

To begin, *the leadership of the corporate church has the
primary responsibility to articulate the strategic vision for the
church-at-large.* Typically, in the centralized organization, leadership is concerned with *how* to get things done, rather than
what the organization should be. Church leaders glow when
they talk about the introduction of long-range planning as
evidence of creative and futuristic thinking. The fact is that
long-range planning tends to focus on the question, How? rather
than, What? Not only can an operational long-range plan based
upon the extension of current conditions become a future credibility trap for leadership, but more important, it can lead an
organization in the direction it does not intend to go, as
Benjamin B. Tregoe and John W. Zimmerman write in their
leadership manual, *Top Management Strategy: What It Is and
How to Make It Work.*

> Strategy is vision directed at *what* the organization
> should be and not *how* the organization will get
> there. We define strategy as *the framework which
> guides those choices that determine the nature and
> direction of an organization.*[5]

Church leaders with a strategic vision will shift their focus
from power and procedures to purpose and product. They will
be able to present a picture of the way the church can look in
the future. This is the vision that inspires people, instills pride,
and engages commitment. Local churches need the sense of being part of a significant movement with an exciting future.

*The corporate church also has the responsibility to communi-
cate, internally and externally, the culture of shared values
which bond together the church-at-large.* In a religious context,
the values are essentially doctrinal, but must also include the
values of being and doing which give the church and its
members their unique identity. A major flaw in the church today

is to assume that the nature of the linkage between the central
and local units is structural rather than doctrinal, behavioral
and cultural. To assume that the integrity of the church can be
maintained by line and staff relationships through which power
flows from top down is a fatal flaw that will be exposed in
the Age of Information. Again, it is the responsibility of top
leadership in the church to articulate the shared values of
doctrine, life, and practice which bond the local ministries
together in purpose, personality, and pride.

McDonald's has something to teach us about communication
through symbols, ceremonies, stories, heroes and even contests
and advertising. Strange isn't it, that in each of these areas,
we fail to capitalize on our strengths for communication? No
organizational culture is richer in symbols, ceremonies, stories
and heroes than the Christian church. Perhaps we have reacted
against the relics and rituals of the Roman Catholic Church.
More likely, we have succumbed to the wiles of secular society,
which has been described as a "land of broken symbols." How
well I remember standing in the restaurant of the Space Needle
high above Seattle, Washington, with Dr. Margaret Mead. As
the restaurant rotated, I pointed out to her the sights of the
city. Suddenly, a brilliant ray of sunlight bounced off a golden
dome on a new building below. Always crisp, Dr. Mead asked,
"What's that?"

I explained, "We are looking at the newest movie theater
in the center of the city."

"Strange," she mused, "we used to reserve our golden
domes for cathedrals, libraries and universities which we placed
high on a hill."

The golden dome of the theater and the golden arches of
McDonald's say much about the search for symbols in our
secular society. Crosses on spires once symbolized our churches,
but now they are buried in modern architecture or they are
meaningless to the modern mind. In the Age of Information,
the corporate church must rediscover the symbols of faith and
our culture. Once in a while, churches try "logos," but they
are soon lost because they do not adequately symbolize the

shared values of the culture or do not adequately represent the strategic vision of the church, around which people will rally. Try as we might, we can think of no symbol of the church today that comes through with the clarity of McDonald's golden arches. We need symbol-makers and story-tellers for the church in the Age of Information.

To continue, *the corporate church must educate the clergy and laity in the vision and values of the religious and spiritual culture.* Ministers of the local church are like the managers of McDonald's franchises. They must be carefully selected and thoroughly prepared to personify the vision and values of the larger church in the local unit. As a seminary president at commencement time, I have looked out often over a graduating class and wondered if we can send them out across the world with the same confidence with which Rome sent out its centurions or McDonald's sends out its managers. The question is not personality, spirituality or professional competence, but whether or not they fully understand the culture of the church and can effectively communicate its primary values.

As a long-time educator in Christian liberal arts colleges, I also see the McDonald's model exposing a weakness in Christian higher education. Hamburger University instills the values of McDonald's culture in its students as well as training them for managerial roles. Admittedly, this is not liberal learning, but value education is not inconsistent with a liberal arts education. How many of our Christian colleges include the teaching of the values of the Christian life and the Christian church culture as a conscious component of their educational mission? Denominational schools, in particular, have a responsibility to inculcate the values of the church culture in their formal and informal curriculums. This does not mean force-fed indoctrination. Learning theory gives us a pattern of value education based upon the principles:

> I prize;
> I choose;
> I act.

Christian higher education has a responsibility to set learning outcomes for its students who will prize, choose and act upon Christian values and the Christian church culture. This is especially true for the future of the local church. Its strength will be found in members who understand, experience and embrace common values of faith and practice.

The corporate church must supply still another resource: a benign but sophisticated information system for research on emerging trends and changing needs at both the church-wide and local levels. If trends move "bottom up," it is essential for the leadership of the corporate church to be aware of the grassroots movement in order to respond. Far less complicated is a demographic census for church membership which can yield surprising and sometimes shaming statistics. As a consultant for a church that wanted to double its membership in a decade through aggressive evangelism, I did a random sample of the membership by age groups and found that the church would meet its goal in less than ten years if just 50 percent of its own youth (which the church was losing), were saved and became members. In another instance, my sister, whose specialty is computers, did a directory of memberships in a local church, which permitted analysis and cross-referencing of data. Her first cut into the information revealed that the church, reputed to be one of the fastest-growing in the nation, actually lost more than 25 percent of its members in one year. Growth came from replacements by the hundreds. Without the efficiency of the computer and the expertise of my sister, that fact (which drove the church to its knees and its ministry into retreat), might never have been known.

Efficiency and expertise are key words for developing information to the benefit of the church. Few local churches can afford the capital and continuing cost of ever-more efficient computers. Nor do they have the expertise required to program the computers for vital information about the church, its people or its community. Here again, the corporate church is an efficient companion to the effectiveness of the local church.

THE LOCAL CHURCH — CENTER FOR ACTION

The local church, then, serves as the center for action:

responding directly to the spiritual needs of people;

serving in the uniqueness of its own local setting with relevant ministries;

communicating through persons and programs the values of the church culture;

utilizing the resources provided by the Hi/Tech center of the corporate body for application in ministry;

identifying with the larger church through its promotion, symbols, and ceremonies;

evangelizing and discipling diverse peoples from the strength of the shared culture;

functioning as the change agent for innovative, need-response ministries;

communicating interests, needs and concerns of the people for the direction and development of the church-at-large; and

contributing to the corporate resource center for services rendered through annual assessments.

The linkage between the corporate resource center and the local church is a senior administrator — usually a regional, conference, or district superintendent — whose task is to serve as a morale builder, troubleshooter and quality controller for pastors. Assessments of pastors and audits of churches are front-edge factors for the church of the future. Pastors are now assessed, but either on the intuition of "It is my impression" or on the rationale of a "Fill-in-the-blanks" questionnaire. Sophisticated instruments are now being developed and tested daily which assess the effectiveness of leadership performance and can be customized for the pastoral role. Audits of churches are quite another thing. How do you measure the effectiveness of a local church? Again, sophisticated techniques can be developed out of management science, cultural studies and biblical princi- ples. Or perhaps we would take a lesson from the regional managers of McDonald's. Assessment is directly related to the clarity, communication and personification of McDonald's values. Through a series of formal and informal testing, a senior manager of McDonald's can determine how a local fran- chise rates on Quality, Service, Convenience and Value. Local churches may include more intangibles which are difficult to measure, but we cannot use a spiritual cop-out to avoid accoun- tability. Jesus did not hesitate to examine churches. How else can we interpret His visits to the seven churches of Asia? The standard of measurement was the faithfulness of the churches to Christ and His Word. Differences among the churches in their local setting were fully respected as influences which had a bearing upon Jesus' judgment. Yet the auditing procedure is standard for each church, not unlike a thorough medical exami- nation. Christ begins with a diagnosis of the spiritual condition of the churches when He reviews their works. A specific pre- scription follows as remedy for its ills.

The examination concludes with a prognosis of spiritual position and power if the church heeds the report and exercises the discipline of change. Why not consider the same procedure for the audit of local churches?

Diagnosis: "I know your works."

Prescription: "Hear the voice of the Spirit."

Prognosis: "To him that overcomes I will give. . ."

Quality control for local churches is almost unknown among us. Yet it is a biblical concept exercised by Christ as the Lord of the church and by Paul as an apostle of churches. Each epistle that Paul wrote reads like a management letter that accompanies an audit report. The status of the church is assessed, critical issues are drawn, and recommendations for improvement are made. Contrary to some opinions, the spiritual effectiveness of churches can be assessed, and it can be improved as a result of that assessment.

Visualize, then, the high-energy church in the Age of Information:

> decentralized in the need-responsive ministries of the local church;

> bonded together in identity with the larger church through a strong culture of faith and practice;

> supported by information, education, and communication of a centralized resource system of the corporate church;

> interconnected in quality with the parent church through the aid and audit of superintending pastors;

> led by national leaders whose task is to communicate the strategic vision and primary values for the past, present, and future of the church.

HE WHO HAS AN EAR, LET HIM HEAR WHAT THE SPIRIT SAYS TO THE CHURCHES.

13.
Hi/Net for Our Evangelism

The Moral Majority is to the future of the Great Commission what McDonald's is to the future of the organized church. Wait. Before rejecting the idea out of hand, remember that the Moral Majority is the first and foremost example of networking outside the church that still involves millions of people in the church. The Moral Majority has something significant to teach us about the role of the church in the Age of Information.

John Naisbitt puts a premium upon the megatrend of movement *from hierarchies to networking* as a result of an information-based society. His fundamental thesis is: Open information in the hands of the masses breaks down the pyramids of hierarchies and builds up networks of communication for social change. Examples known to all of us include the networks which carry the causes of feminism, abortion, gay rights, consumer protection and political accountability. Networks also carry counter-causes against abortion, pornography, nuclear arms, drunk driving, perverted musical lyrics, and feminism. Usually, however, they are framed in positive terms, such as pro-life, pro-family, pro-morality, pro-American, pro-defense and pro-Israel. Other networks are more benign. SOLINET, the computerized network, interconnects the libraries of the nation, and HOLINET, the satellite network, links Holiday Inns across the world for tele-conferencing in their meeting rooms.

NETWORKING DEVELOPS WHEN HIERARCHIES FAIL TO RESPOND TO CHANGING HUMAN NEEDS AND RISING MORAL CONCERNS.

The networking with which we are concerned is not benign. Rather, it represents a new configuration of human interaction based upon information. By nature, hierarchies

> slow down the flow of information;
> respond sluggishly to changing needs; and
> limit conversation to formal channels.

But when information comes openly and directly to people, they begin to talk to each other outside the hierarchical structure. If the new information rouses a common need to which the hierarchy cannot or does not respond, the instruments of mass communication, from the telephone to the satellite, become the means for diverse peoples with a common concern to talk and act together.

The Moral Majority is a creation of information. In 1964, the March on Selma for black rights prompted Jerry Falwell to preach a sermon against Christian involvement in political issues. Fifteen years later, he skyrocketed into celebrity status as the leader of a loosely-connected national organization that was dedicated to Christian involvement in political affairs. How can we account for Jerry Falwell's apparent flip-flop in position with both sides justified by biblical mandate? In a conversation with him, I asked the question. He thought a moment and then answered, "The Supreme Court decision on abortion in 1973. Then and there, I knew that I had to get involved."

A classic case study of networking follows. With the Supreme Court decision came massive and often conflicting volumes of information about abortion and its consequences. The nation literally chose up sides in the debate. Yet, the traditional hierarchies of religion, education, and politics were paralyzed in place. They were too slow in helping their constituents digest the information, and slower yet in presenting positions that were responsive to the need. Therefore, Jerry Falwell discovered a national constituency of millions that spread across religious, social, economic and political lines. Diverse as they were, the people shared one common concern — the right to life. Criticize Jerry Falwell if you will, but commend him for capturing the tide of networking in the dawning Age of Information.

NETWORKING DEVELOPS WHEN SHARED INFORMATION GIVES POWER FOR DIVERSE PEOPLE TO TAKE POSITIONS ON MORALLY AMBIGUOUS ISSUES.

Networking develops not just when hierachies are slow to respond to new information and changing needs, but also under certain conditions in the environment. First, *ambiguity* clouds the issue, especially in the moral realm. Second, *diverse masses* of people who fit no traditional organization are concerned about the issue or the need. Third, *relevant information* has the potential for positioning on the issue or addressing the need. Under these conditions, the person or the group that defines the loosely connected goals of diverse people, provides the relevant information, and opens the communication system for them to talk and act will have created a network that can change an institution or influence a nation.

To understand the difference between hierarchies and networking, the following comparison is helpful:

HIERARCHIES Tend toward:	NETWORKING Tends toward:
Static structure (noun)	Dynamic connections (verb)
Elitism	Egalitarianism
Efficiency	Effectiveness

Two-dimensionality	Three-dimensionality
(up and down)	(up, down, horizontal)
Homogeneity	Heterogeneity
Stability	Change
Transfer of knowledge	Creation of knowledge
Channeled communication	Open communication
Status	Belonging
System-orientation	People-orientation

Admittedly, these distinctions are overstated. Hierarchies can be creative agents for communication and change and networks can be disguises for hierarchical control. Just as in the case of the megashift toward decentralization, it is not an either/or choice. As we consider the future of the church, we need the stability of hierarchies complemented by the flexibility of networks.

NETWORKS NEED HIERARCHIES
TO AVOID THE TEMPTATION
TO BECOME HIERARCHIES THEMSELEVES.

In my book, *Renewing Our Ministry,* I cite the analogy used by Peter Drucker to distinguish two extremes of organizational structure.[1] One extreme is the computer which is internally rigid in structure. It has no sensitivity to its external environment and responds only according to the instructions that are fed into it. The computer is a genius in efficiency, but an imbecile in effectiveness. The other extreme is the amoeba, an organism that has no internal structure but constantly changes shape in reponse to stimuli from the external environment. The amoeba is a genius in effectiveness, but an imbecile in efficiency.

In its extreme form, the computer is like a hierarchy and the amoeba is like a network. Naisbitt tends to put them into either/or categories. He misses the values that each contributes to an organization and to a society. Most of all, he misses the meaning of the Body of Christ which is the biblical anatomy for the function of the church. An organic body combines the internal structure of the computer with the external sensitivity of the amoeba. Still the analogy fails without the mystery of life itself. As we consider the future role of the church, we cannot fix on either hierarchies or networks as the ideal we embrace. Only the Body of Christ with its mystery of life suffices for us. Why, then, do we continue to move toward hierarchical structures patterned after the organizations of the Industrial Age? If we protect that pattern in the Age of Information, we will see the hierarchical church falling into obsolescence, while multiple ministries spin off into new orbits through the dynamics of networking.

NETWORKS ARE THE PARACHURCH MINISTRIES OF THE AGE OF INFORMATION.

In the post-World War II years of the twentieth century, we saw the spectacular rise of what has euphemistically been called "parachurch ministries," such as Youth for Christ, InterVarsity Fellowship, Young Life and Campus Crusade. Essentially, they were created in response to the knowledge and the need of the post-war baby boom. Traditional church structures, including hierarchies, did not process the information or respond to the need with the speed and flexibility required to take the gospel to youth rather than waiting for them to come to the church. Without doubt, the hierarchy of the church was threatened, and not always without reason. Even today, the debate continues over the relationship of parachurch organizations to denominations and local churches. Yet, if the facts were known, parachurch ministries may well have been the catalysts for the "Born-again" movement of the 1970s from which evangelical churches benefited by spiritual renewal, numerical growth and public visibility.

The tension between the church and parachurch ministries is now giving way to the common threat of networks sophisticated in the use of the media and sensitive to changing needs that are not being met by either the church or parachurch organizations. While the Moral Majority is the prototype, it has already given way to federations, coalitions, councils and congresses. These cross the boundaries of churches with moral issues such as abortion, theological positions such as inerrancy, and spiritual experiences such as charismatic gifts. *Time* magazine also reports that TV evangelists, while appearing to compete for viewers and dollars, constitute a network within networks because they share a common viewpoint.[2] Almost without exception, the electronic church is evangelical or fundamentalist. Four of its top personalities are Pentecostal; their viewers cluster in the sun belt and their politics tip heavily toward the right. The power of what is called the "Jesus network" is mind-boggling — 3 major broadcast networks, 200 local TV stations, 1,134 radio stations, freelance media productions, cable and satellite hookups worth billions of dollars in equipment, air time and expenses!

Again, whatever criticism we may have for gospel TV, we cannot deny that it is a creation of the Age of Information. Into the moral and spiritual ambiguity of electronic media, television preachers have filled the void between the traditional church and the changing needs of diversified people.

HIERARCHIES NEED NETWORKS; NETWORKS NEED HIERARCHIES.

In *Megatrends,* Naisbitt sees hierarchies breaking down and networks building up as the organizational pattern for the future. He misses the point that networks need hierarchies and hierarchies need networks. They are interdependent. Hierarchies without networks tend toward authoritarianism; networks without hierarchies tend toward anarchy. Therefore, as we contemplate the role of the church in the Age of Information, we must foresee the potential of the Body of Christ as a divinely-ordained and Spirit-motivated creation. At its balanced best, the Body of Christ fully utilizes the strengths of the skeletal structure in coordination with the sensitivities of the external organs, with Christ as the Head.

Jesus put these Body principles into practice when He commissioned us:

> All authority has been given to Me in heaven and
> on earth. Go therefore and make disciples of all

nations, baptizing them in the name of the Father and of the Son and of the Holy Spirit, teaching them to observe all things that I have commanded you; and lo, I am with you always, even to the end of the age (Matthew 28:18-20, NKJV).

Within His words are the components for networking the Great Commission. In fact, without networking, the Great Commission will not be realized.

"Go" assumes a world environment that is uncertain and ambiguous;

"all nations" assumes the diversity of peoples and the magnitude of the masses; and

"make disciples" assumes the potential power of revelant information.

Two inescapable facts confront us. One is the astounding realization that, for the first time, the information revolution has put in our hands the means by which the Great Commission can be fulfilled. The other is the sobering revelation that we can never fulfill the Great Commission through the agencies of hierarchies alone.

Three components make up the Great Commission network:

the preaching media;
the teaching church; and
the baptizing link.

Everyone who accepts the Great Commission has a responsibility for the full and total development of each person who is in Christ. Personal conversion is the task of the preaching media; public confession is the purpose of the baptizing link; and Christian maturity is the goal of the teaching church. Local churches are microcosms of the Great Commission network because they have ministries for each component. They cannot, however, fulfill their responsibility for the Great Commission in local isolation. With the coming of the electronic church, they become one or two of the components in the network for the evangelization of the world. Likewise, the preaching media as represented by gospel TV cannot fulfill the functions of the baptizing link and the teaching church as well as the local church can. Therefore, the electronic church and the local church are inseparably connected in mutual responsibility that has come to them out of the Age of Information. Three premises follow:

> The preaching media can be expanded world-wide through electronic communications;
>
> the teaching church can best be achieved through local ministries; and
>
> the baptizing link requires the creation of a new transitional ministry between the preaching media and the teaching church.

Each of these components of the Great Commission network deserves individual attention.

From the field of electricity, we better understand the meaning of networking. An electric network is designed specifically for the purpose of increasing the amount of electricity that can be carried without overloading the system. This is done through the electrical impact of one body on the other without touching. Resistance is reduced, induction is increased, and capacity is multiplied. Is not this our goal for Christian ministries in order to fulfill the Great Commission? If either gospel TV or the local church tries without the other to fulfill the Great Commission, the system is overloaded. But if we can make a positive impact of one upon the other without the formal connection of organizational structure, we can reduce the negative resistance, increase the positive influence, and multiply the capacity of the system. To carry the gospel to the ends of the earth and make disciples of all nations without overloading the system is the end to which the church in the Age of the Information must be committed.

THE PREACHING MEDIA —
"GO AND MAKE DISCIPLES OF ALL NATIONS."

Imagine an international network for communicating the gospel of Jesus Christ that penetrates into the spiritual ambiguity of world systems and reaches across the lines of cultural diversity. A few years ago, the Genesis Project carried that dream. The intention was to produce the drama of the Bible on film with the Scripture as the only text, translated into the language of viewers of every nation and dialect. The Genesis Project faltered, but the idea must be kept alive. Almost every Sunday on television you can hear an evangelist speak the vision of taking the gospel to the whole world. But it is always in the context of his or her own television ministry. No single network or television program can fulfill the Great Commission. If TV evangelists, denominational executives and parachurch leaders are serious in their desire to win the world, they must come together in creating a cooperative network designed exclusively for world evangelism. Obviously, a monolithic structure is not only undesirable, but impossible. If, however, there were an international consortium for world evangelism perhaps under the aegis of a Great Commission network which utilized the untold resources entrusted into the hands of evangelicals, the potential would be unlimited. Studies of networking show that none of the traditional forms of planning, organizing, staffing and controlling are effective. Instead, a leader who effectively utilizes a network provides a map rather than a rulebook, exercises persuasion rather than power, stresses belonging rather than status, and has a singular common goal rather than multiple objectives. Idealistic? Of course, but so is the Great Commission.

THE TEACHING CHURCH —
"TEACHING THEM TO OBSERVE ALL THINGS
THAT I HAVE COMMANDED YOU."

We must be quick to recognize that the task of teaching new Christians all of the things that Jesus has commanded us can best be done through the ministry of the local church. To assume that a person can come to spiritual maturity through the impersonal or independent study of the Word of God is a contradiction of Scripture. Teaching in the New Testament following the baptism of believers was a corporate experience with learning that included:

> instruction in doctrine;
> participating in fellowship;
> breaking of bread; and
> practice of prayer (Acts 2:41-47).

Furthermore, we remember how the Holy Spirit sent Philip to the chariot of the powerful and intelligent Ethiopian eunuch who was reading Isaiah alone. Philip asked him, "Do you understand what you are reading?"

The Ethiopian answered, "How can I, unless someone guides me?"

Philip opened the Word to him and preached Jesus. The man believed and was baptized on the spot.

Without the corporate, personalized and total learning experience of the teaching church, newly converted and baptized believers cannot come to spiritual maturity. However sophisticated the Hi/Tech of the preaching media may become, it will never be a substitute for the Lo/Tech learning environment of the local church.

Neither the electronic church nor the local church has learned the fundamental lesson of communications for world evangelism. At the present time, they are almost mutually exclusive. Even though a study done by the Annenburg School of Communications at the University of Pennsylvania finds that gospel TV does not undercut attendance and contributions in the local church, the suspicion remains. A bumper sticker on behalf of the local church reads, "ROBERT SCHULLER DOESN'T MAKE HOUSE CALLS." Certainly, the weakness of Schuller's ministry is exposed. But to be fair, the other side of the bumper should carry the sticker, "ROBERT SCHULLER

PREACHES TO MILLIONS." Then, we would have identified the complementary strengths of the electronic church and the local church. Preaching is an announcement made for the media; teaching is a process made for the local church.

During my sabbatical at Cambridge University, I sat at tea with Professor Gordon Rupp, one of the world's foremost historians of the eighteenth-century Wesleyan Revival in England. Historians are especially cautious about making connections between one century and another. Yet I took the chance of a scholar's rebuff by asking the question, "If John Wesley were alive today, would he use television for his preaching?"

With the certainty of his years of study, Professor Rupp instantly answered, "Yes, by all means."

He knew that the man who took to the fields and the market place to preach to the masses would be on television today.

Wesley, however, would bring a new dimension to television preaching. In the field and in the marketplace, he got the attention of the masses by announcing the gospel and then inviting his hearers to a class meeting where they would hear more about salvation and be converted to Jesus Christ. Wesley never intended to start a church or pretended to fulfill the preaching, baptizing and teaching tasks of the Great Commission by himself. The primary purpose of the class meeting was to prepare converts for taking communion and participating in the worship of the local church. In contemporary terms, Wesley created the class meeting as a "halfway house" between his preaching to the masses and the teaching of the church for those who came to Christ.

What a far cry from the current scene. With a few notable exceptions, gospel TV reaches the masses, but makes no connection with the local church. In turn, many local churches serve as pastor to people, but make no connection with the converts of gospel TV. Why? I suspect that the snarls in the network are carnal. Gospel TV is so expensive and the pressure for funding is so intense that its preachers fear the loss of revenues if their converts make a commitment to the local church. The local church, on the other hand, tends to be a group of homogeneous people who have difficulty absorbing converts who are not of their own kind. A follow-up study of Billy Graham's New York Crusades confirms this observation. The decisions for Christ were found to be genuine, but most of the converts never made the transition to the local church. Even though the names of converts were sent to local churches, the system failed because there was little transitional ministry between the Crusade and the local church. Even more significant, there was little provision in the ministry of the local church for bringing into membership persons who were not its own converts or of its own kind.

THE BAPTIZING LINK — "BAPTIZING THEM IN THE NAME OF THE FATHER AND OF THE SON AND OF THE HOLY SPIRIT."

How many times have you heard television preachers encourage their converts to seek out a local church? How many times have you heard your local pastors ask how the church can minister to the masses who hear the gospel via television? The preaching media and the teaching church need the baptizing link. Baptism is the public act of confession of faith in Jesus Christ. A call to an 800 number with follow-up literature is not the public confession that is needed after personal conversion. As it is, the faceless connector with a voice on the telephone lends itself to the privatism of religion which we have already defined as a greater threat to the church than the secularization of society. Somehow, some way, the public confession of the baptizing link must become an effective connector between the preaching media and the teaching church. This can be accomplished through beginning and expanding the following activities:

> Create an evangelical network through which the preaching media shares the names of converts for follow-up by the local church.

Establish a computerized follow-up system for serving preaching media converts.

Issue a public invitation from the local church for converts of the preaching media to enter into their fellowship.

Prepare tapes and books on Christian doctrine and discipleship which connect the preaching media and the teaching church.

Utilize parachurch ministry, Bible study, and prayer groups as "halfway" ministries between the preaching media and the local church.

Encourage teaching church members to serve as volunteers for the preaching media in the local community.

Publish a directory of ministries provided by local churches as a community resource.

Establish in each community a well-publicized, single-access number for inquirers and converts to call for referrals to match their spiritual status and needs.

In our United Way study of human service needs in the Greater Bluegrass Region of Kentucky, we found that people with problems did not know where to go and agencies with services did not know what other agencies were doing. A survey of the parents of pre-school handicapped children, for instance, showed that they were suffering from the lack of information about their child's handicap and were frustrated because they did not know whom to call. A parallel survey of human service agencies in the community which served handicapped children revealed that the resources were available but not on a cooperative basis. Voluntarily, then, the agencies came together and proposed a community awareness program backed up by a single-access number which parents could call for information and referral. More and more, we are learning that the magnitude

and intensity of human service needs can be addressed only
through full community cooperation and a point of public access
between needs and services.

The church in the Age of Information is confronted with
the same challenge. Resources of the church must be matched
with the needs of people. The preaching media has the resources
to reach millions; teaching churches have the resources to
disciple hundreds of thousands. Yet, each seems to be attempting
to fulfill the Great Commission alone through hierarchical structures. The gospel suffers; people suffer. Evangelical Christians
have already discovered the power of networking in the political
arena. Why not find a way to utilize and expand this creative
complement for world evangelism, church growth and cooperative ministries?

**NETWORKING IS A GIFT TO THE CHURCH
FROM THE AGE OF INFORMATION FOR THE
FULFILLMENT OF THE GREAT COMMISSION.**

14.
Hi/Power for Our Leadership

Buckminster Fuller, father of the geodesic dome and one of the most fertile minds of the twentieth century, envisioned a day when mankind would be governed by a world democracy. The franchise of "one person — one vote" would be extended to every human being on earth. Via satellite, issues of the world state would be communicated, debated and decided by electronic vote. Lightning-fast computers would then count billions of ballots and announce the majority decision. Of course, political elections and legislative sessions of representative government would be obsolete. A world referendum would make the decisions that legislatures now make, but on a global scale — regarding human rights, military budgets, environmental protection and economic policy. Political action would be reduced to one grand, global lobbying effort. Thus, Bucky Fuller fantasizes the ideal of participatory democracy with every person directly involved in world decisions. The dream is intriguing but the reality is frightening.

In *Megatrends,* John Naisbitt is on the same track, but running at a slower pace and toward a lesser goal. He projects a megashift from representative democracy to participatory democracy in the Age of Information. In tracing the trend, he presents the evidence that citizen initiatives and legislative referenda are now commonplace in our governing process. The case of Proposition 13 in California is cited as the forerunner of participatory democracy. Californians rebelled against increased taxes without proportional benefits. Gathering information to prove their case, the people voted limits on property taxes and forced the state to live within its means. Proposition 13 encouraged other citizen groups to take issues of government into their own hands. As we noted earlier, people rally around issues that directly affect their welfare. More often than not, citizen initiatives center on such single-interest issues as nuclear energy, environmental protection, pornography, state lotteries, nursing home regulations, seat belt laws and, of course, property taxes and school bonding. Whenever citizens do not like what is going on in government or want to force the hand of their elected representatives, they petition for an initiative. Likewise, whenever legislators want to skirt their responsibility on delicate decisions, they encourage a referendum.

WE ARE LIVING WITH THE RESULTS OF WHAT IS CALLED "THE SAGEBRUSH REBELLION."

In the mid-1970s, the legislature of Washington state was heavily lobbied by commercial interests to pass laws reversing the prohibition of gambling. Everyone got into the act. Firemen, senior citizens and the Roman Catholic Church supported bingo; hotel, restaurant and tavern owners pleaded for pull tabs and card games; the syndicated Eastern gambling establishment put on pressure for slot machines and casino games; and the politicians drooled at the thought of state-wide lottery as a way to avoid tax increases. No one in the legislature, however, dared to take the lead for fear of political consequences at election time. So the legislature called for a public referendum to determine the will of the people. The majority favored laws permitting games of chance, but the vote did not specify the type of games or the extent of gambling. Governor Daniel J. Evans stepped in to establish a blue-ribbon committee charged with the responsibility of studying gambling and making recommendations to him. To my surprise and discomfort, he called and asked me — a non-gambling clergyman and a non-political educator — to chair the committee. When I asked him why he chose me, the governor answered, "The people voted to liberalize gambling, but caution is needed; and we are concerned about the quality of life in our state. We want a man with good credentials in whom the public has confidence."

A long story follows. With fear and trembling, I accepted the position as a responsibility of my citizenship and my Christian witness. In the crossfire of conflicting political, economic and moral demands, the objectivity of factual information carried the case against casino gambling and a state lottery. Social gambling, such as bingo and card games without a professional dealer, were allowed under the scrutiny of a gambling commission, but with the caution that cheating, corruption and crime are threats at every level where big dollars are at stake in games of chance. As chairman of the committee, I wrote a minority report opposing gambling as a "non-productive, parasitic" enterprise which corrupts our quality of life by creating a climate in which people expect to "get something for nothing." Our recommendations prevailed to become the law of the state until the early 1980s when another citizen referendum called for a state-wide lottery as an alternative to a tax increase.

THE SPIRIT OF PROPOSITION 13 LIVES ON!

Democracy thrives when informed and concerned citizens get involved in the political process. Alexis de Tocqueville, the French historian, discovered the genius of American democracy in the image of a pioneer heading into the wilderness with the Bible and a newspaper in one hand and an ax in the other. Today, the image might be the citizen commuting to work with a TV in one hand and a computer in the other. Information does make a difference in governance. The more information people have, the more they expect to be involved and consulted in the decision-making process. Information also increases accountability. In the Age of Information, we can expect that representatives of the people will be constantly called to account for their decisions.

Naisbitt goes a step further. He assumes that the accumulation of information in the hands of the masses will render obsolete the kind of representative democracy that we now know. Already, he says,

> it doesn't matter who is President of the United States;
> Congress is obsolete;
> the two-party system is dead; and
> Washington, D.C., is no longer the center of power.

He may be right, but if so, it means that we have lost the values of representative government which can never be found in a full-scale system of participatory democracy. One value is the *authority* invested in persons on whom we depend to be knowledgeable of the law, concerned for our welfare, protective of our rights and pledged to preserve the nation. Even though we have so often heard "a million Frenchmen can't be wrong," we know that at times the majority may not be right. But if the majority is wrong, whom do we hold accountable?

Another value that is endangered by participatory democracy is the *trust* that we put into our elected representatives. To assume that we trust no one but ourselves is to deny the interdependence of human relationships and confess that we do not trust ourselves either.

Still another loss is the assurance of a *point of control*. De Tocqueville said that both the strengths and weaknesses of American democracy arise from the frequency of popular elections by which citizens can change leaders and put the other party into power. If, as Naisbitt suggests, elected leadership and the two-party system are incidental or dead, we lose the leverage of our executive, judicial and legislative check-and-balance system. The point of control shifts, then, to the image, impression and interpretation of an issue as communicated by the media. All of the evils of Orwell's *Nineteen Eighty-Four* spill out of that Pandora's box.

LEADERSHIP IS NOT EITHER/OR.

In the book, *Leaders: Strategies for Taking Charge,* by Warren Bennis and Burt Nanus, we are introduced to a changing view of leadership that breaks away from the outmoded models related to personality, power and position. Instead, the authors describe four qualitative aspects of leadership which are essential to involving followers in the task of the enterprise. Also, rather than beginning with the organizational setting of which the leader is a part, Bennis and Nanus begin with the qualities of the person who leads. The working principle is pointedly defined in the title of the chapter, "Leading Others: Managing Yourself."[1]

FIRST, THE LEADER ENGAGES COMMITMENT THROUGH A FOCUSED VISION.

A vision that is too general cannot be grasped, while a vision that is too specific cannot fire the imagination. Someplace in between is the balance of genius. A critical indicator is the confidence that followers have in the leader. As one person said about his leader, "He knows what he wants and doesn't waste our time." Not only must the vision be significant for the organization, but each person must find a significant role to play in its achievement.

SECOND, THE LEADER GIVES MEANING THROUGH COMMUNICATION.

Communication is a *shibboleth* that is used to explain why things go wrong in an organization. The tendency is to open, repair and revise the formal lines of communication. But something is wrong. The problem may not be the system of communication, but the substance of communication. Unless "meaning" is conveyed through communication, no amount of time spent in participatory leadership will suffice. Meaning, in this sense, is significance. A fatal error is to assume that information is synonymous with meaning in organizational communication. To the contrary, Robert Townsend, in his pithy book, *Up the Organization,* diagnoses the dangers of a leadership malady called "murder by memo."[2] One danger is to assume that the number of memos is directly proportional to the interpretation of meaning among employees or followers. The other danger is to assume that memos are substitutes for face-to-face communication. Studies of effective leaders reveal that they spend a lot of time talking about incidentals with their subordinates. In fact, their conversation tends to be more playful then instructive. Yet, through stories, symbols, similies, analogies and jokes, they communicate meaning which makes their followers feel that they are engaged in a significant task.

THIRD, THE LEADERS CREATE TRUST THROUGH POSITIONING.

Caught in the crossfire of conflicting information, people need constancy of leadership. President Ronald Reagan modeled this quality. Whether you agreed with his policies or not, you always knew where he stood. In White House briefings, his answers to questions could be anticipated before he gave them. His motto, "Stay on course," was a master stroke of leadership positioning. The payoff was public trust. As strange as it seems, public opinion gave him high marks for leadership at the same time that opposition was mounting against his policies. Evidently, people can separate the person of the President from his policies. Constancy is the secret. Trust is the result. President Jimmy Carter probably knew more about the issues of office than Ronald Reagan, but once he got the reputation for vacillation, he lost the trust of the people long before he lost his bid for re-election.

Fred Smith, an astute reader of people and organizations, believes that he has discovered the secret of success for television preachers and evangelical celebrities. "They never get out of role," he reasons. Fred then points out examples: "You can always count on Robert Schuller being Robert Schuller, Oral Roberts being Oral Roberts, and Pat Robertson being Pat

Robertson." It is the leader who frequently shifts roles or changes position who creates distrust.

Constancy and trust are well-illustrated in the Peanuts cartoon. Whenever Charlie Brown tries to fly the kite of his aspirations, he invariably snags it on the same pesky tree. But when Charlie Brown is weary and discouraged, it is the same antagonistic tree against which he puts his head and says, "A tree is not only good for shade from the sun and keeping the rain off our head, but in times of trouble, it is also very good to lean against." The analogy of the cross as our scandal and support is inescapably clear in this cartoon, but more than that, it reminds us of the constancy of Christ. His leadership snags our aspirations at times, but we can always count upon His never-failing presence in our time of need.

FOURTH, THE LEADER EMPOWERS OTHERS THROUGH SELF-DEPLOYMENT.

In classic leadership theory, a superior-subordinate relationship is defined by the lines and boxes of authority, power, titles and functions. This is like trying to describe a person by showing the skeleton without flesh and blood, mind and spirit, thoughts and feelings. Therefore, current leadership studies center on the person in interaction with other persons. Bennis and Nanus, for instance, find that persons who are leaders vary on a broad spectrum of personalities and styles, but have in common a strong sense of self-worth or what they call "positive self-regard." No mystery veils this quality. Bennis and Nanus report that positive self-regard is the result of a leader

recognizing his or her strengths and weaknesses;

capitalizing on the strengths and compensating for the weaknesses; and

matching strengths with the task to be done.[3]

From this working base, a leader dares to take risks and learn from failure. What is called "The Wallenda factor" is

introduced into leadership theory. Karl Wallenda, father of the
family troupe that defied death on the high wire, once said,

> To be on the high wire is living. Everything else is
> waiting.

Wallenda's wife remembers that her husband never thought
about falling during all of the years of his career — until his
last act. For the first time, she recalls that he worried about
the wire and expressed his fear of falling. As if acting out his
premonitions, Wallenda failed, fell and died. When he lost his
positive self-regard, he lost his life.

Positive self-regard is even more significant for leadership
than being able to take a risk and learn from failure. *A person
in a leadership position with positive self-regard can give himself
away!* Bennis and Nanus speak about the "deployment of self"
in tasks and relationships above and beyond oneself. The motto
of Rotary International comes to mind: Service Above Self.
Only a person with positive self-regard has the security for
self-extension. Otherwise, self-protection, self-aggrandizement
and self-justification are the dominant motives.

One of the surprises of the *Fortune Magazine* annual listing
of the 400 wealthiest people is to find that they are also
recognized as the hardest working people in their business or
organization. For each of us who will never make the Fortune
400, we dream of the luxury and leisure that wealth provides.
To gain or hold that wealth, however, requires a deployment
of self in time and energy. Whether the motive is money or
ministry, leaders are people who give themselves away.

Self-deployment from positive self-regard is a power of its
own. Bennis and Nanus find that leaders who give themselves
away empower others to give themselves away as well.[4] Although
that purpose fits either a secular or spiritual setting, its basis
is biblical. Jesus said it first, "He who saves his life shall lose
it; and he who loses his life for My sake and the gospel shall
save it." Whether the rewards are temporal or eternal, the principle holds. To deploy oneself in a task from a position of positive self-regard is to empower others to deploy themselves in

their tasks. Together, then, the goals of the organization are achieved.

CLERGY WHO LEAD
WILL HAVE LAITY WHO PARTICIPATE.

Leading others by managing yourself applies directly to the leadership role of the clergy in the Age of Information. With the decline of clerical authority based upon professional knowledge or positional power, the clergy needs the compensatory authority that comes from the instrumentality of vision, communication, positioning and self-deployment. Commitment, meaning, trust and empowerment result from effective pastoral leadership that bridges the ages of Agriculture, Industry and Information, through the styles of transforming or transactional leadership, into the system of democracy, whether representative or participatory.

Again, we must acknowledge the shift of laity expectations toward participatory democracy in the church with the coming of the Age of Information. The four leadership strategies for taking charge are not inconsistent with more participation by laity in the governing and ministry of the church. Yet, neither the clergy nor the laity can let representative or participatory leadership style become ends in themselves. Our common, singular goal must be the full empowerment of both clergy and laity to be effective ministers in their own sphere of influence. Participatory democracy can be an aid to that end. Ted Engstrom and Ed Dayton, in their newsletter *Christian Leadership,* give us four working principles for participatory democracy which are directly applicable to clergy-laity relationships in the church.[5]

FIRST, PARTICIPATORY LEADERSHIP
SHOULD BE EXERCISED IF THE PEOPLE CAN
CONTRIBUTE KNOWLEDGE TO THE PLANNING
AND DECISION-MAKING PROCESS.

A few years ago, I was asked to chair a long-range planning committee for my denomination. I accepted the assignment on the condition that I could tap the expertise of our laity across the nation. A quick survey caused me to realize how rich we were in people with knowledge and perspective that the church needed, but how poor we were in recognizing and utilizing these invaluable resources. We discovered persons who were responsible for strategic and long-range planning for cities and corporations, schools and shopping malls, hospitals and hotels. Names of computer experts, management consultants, corporate executives, demographers, urban planners, personnel directors, advertising managers, newscasters, legislators and educators came to mind in the first brain-storming session. Regrettably, the process broke down because funding did not follow the idea. Yet, we learned that we should never engage in planning without the participation of our laity who knew more about the process than we did.

SECOND, PARTICIPATORY LEADERSHIP SHOULD BE EXERCISED WHEN THE PROCESS PROVIDES AN OPPORTUNITY FOR THE LAITY TO LEARN.

Expertise and experience are not just on the side of the laity. Clergy also have something to teach their people. Theology, for instance, is a conundrum to many lay people. Through participatory leadership, the pastor can teach how to integrate biblical theology with other disciplines in the planning process. For instance, demographics may assure the growth of the church in a new location, but the biblical mandate may put serving human need above growing as a church. The complexity of church governance is equally perplexing because the system depends upon volunteers who can leave at any time. Pastoral care is another area of ministry that lay people expect but may not understand. When a pastor is struggling with issues in these areas, wisdom suggests that the laity might profitably be engaged for the contribution of their perspective and the benefit of their understanding. Especially when a pastor is trying to change a church or cultivate a new generation of laity, participatory leadership is an invaluable teaching/learning tool.

THIRD, PARTICIPATORY LEADERSHIP
SHOULD BE EXERCISED
WHEN IT IS ESSENTIAL TO CREATE OWNERSHIP
IN A DECISION OR DEMONSTRATE OPENNESS
IN THE DECISION-MAKING PROCESS.

A leader's ability to lead is directly related to the extent to which followers "buy into" his vision, plans and decisions. Situations vary. At critical times, a leader can make a decision without consultation and receive affirmation from the people. At other times, the scene is so sensitive that a leader must prepare to put all other things aside and pull out all stops in the participatory process.

Out of my experience, I remember a decision made by a board of trustees about which the faculty felt that they had not been adequately consulted. Therefore, the faculty refused to accept ownership for the new program that the decision spawned. When I arrived on the scene, my first action was to restart the process by creating a task force of trustees, faculty, administration, staff, students and alumni representatives, and by calling for a three-day consultation. It helped, but it did not solve the problem. Faculty representatives to the task force accepted only conditional ownership of the idea, and those who did not participate still felt as if they had not been adequately consulted. Participatory leadership came too late.

Ownership is often a matter of timing. Findings from a study I made for my doctoral dissertation show that faculty members want participation in goal-setting and planning for their academic departments, but then they want their administrator to implement their goals and plans in organizing, staffing, directing, coordinating, budgeting and reporting so that they can get on with their teaching and research. The key, of course, is timing. Participatory leadership in a university or a church is most essential in the initial stages of goal-setting and planning. No end of grief is saved by following this simple rule. I know from experience.

FOURTH, PARTICIPATORY LEADERSHIP
SHOULD BE EXERCISED
TO INVOLVE THE PEOPLE WHOSE WELFARE
IS DIRECTLY AFFECTED BY THE DECISION.

Not everyone has to be involved in participatory democracy at all times. A student who disagreed with a decision I had made said, "Your decision has caused division among us. This is not pleasing to God. I believe that He wants us to make our decisions in this institution as the Body of Christ by 100 percent agreement after discussion and prayer." My response was not too charitable. After reminding him of the fact that the Acts of the Apostles would have been stalled in Jerusalem if there had been 100 percent agreement about the evangelistic strategy of the church, I cited the division of labor in the Body of Christ as defined in Paul's first letter to the Corinthian church.

Then, perhaps with overkill, I turned a community forum into a classroom by explaining the principle of consultation with the people whose welfare or task is directly affected by the pending decision. In this particular case, I had been assured of consultation through the administrator of the department. Later, after the unpopular decision ignited student ire, I realized that I should have gone personally to the faculty whose lives were involved. Without face-to-face communications with the president, they were informed but not consulted.

More often than not, two, three, or all of these reasons for participatory leadership converge with urgency and value. In the Age of Information, the expectations for participatory leadership will spill over from the society-at-large into the governance of the church through the expectations of the laity. To presume, however, that it is the only style of leadership to be exercised in the Age of Information is to undermine the legitimate authority of the clergy and reduce the effective Body of Christ to a useless blob.

Depending upon the timing and the circumstances, the clerical leader must know when to pronounce, "Thus saith the Lord," and when to ask, "What is your opinion?" In each case, rather than relying upon status, symbols and sanctity as the power for leadership, the pastor will rely upon the primary authority of the Word of God complemented by the personal qualities of leadership in response to laity needs:

Pastoral leadership	*Laity response*
Focused vision	Personal commitment
Effective communication	Meaning
Constancy of position	Trust
Deployment of self	Empowerment

Hi/Power for the leadership of the church in the Age of Information is a spirit-guided balance between an authoritative clergy and a participating laity. The fulcrum is a leadership strategy for deployment of self from a basis of positive self-regard, with the singular purpose of empowering the laity to give themselves away. Jesus gives us our example when He so empowers His disciples as to be able to say,

GREATER WORKS THAN THESE
SHALL YOU DO.

15.
Hi/Tone for Our Witness

More than two hundred years ago, a young man with the sophisticated bearing of an Oxford don climbed the steps of a stone monument called the "market cross" in the industrial ghetto of Liverpool, England. Leaning against the cross and looking out over the milling masses, his eyes and ears were shocked by the sights and sounds of dirty and bedraggled miners and millers venting the rage of their hopelessness with damning curses and drunken brawls.

Breathing a prayer and stretching tall against the cross, the young man began to sing,

> O, for a thousand tongues to sing,
> My great Redeemer's praise,
> The glories of my God and King,
> The triumphs of His grace.

The words came easily from his lips because he had written them to celebrate the first anniversary of his conversion to Jesus Christ. He had no trouble with the music because he sang in the melody of a popular tune which all of the people would recognize. Wafting over the market square like a clarion

call, the song brought an abrupt halt to the bickering and brawl-
ing masses. Never before had they heard a note of joy in a religious context. To them, the church meant a sober sound reserved
for saints and sanctuaries. To them, religion meant a division
between the saved and the damned, with little doubt about
their eternal position. To them, God was a great watch-maker
in the sky who wound up the world and left it running without
a whit of care for His own creation.

No wonder Charles Wesley got their attention. He sang of
a God of love who offered free grace for all through His Son
Jesus Christ. Joy is the only tone that can carry that message.
Before the silent and subdued masses, then, another small,
scholarly figure climbed up the stairs to the cross. John Wesley
preached what his brother Charles sang. Out of this setting,
the Wesleyan Revival was born and England was transformed
in the eighteenth century.

Megatrends ends with a shout, "My God, what a fantastic
time to be alive!" John Naisbitt is not a Christian. His hope
comes from the New Age philosophy which is built upon confidence in an ever-rising human consciousness. As we noted
earlier, this is a spiritualized form of the evolutionary theory
in which mankind is automatically, selectively and inevitably
destined to higher and higher levels of human spirit and achievement. Naisbitt leaves no doubt about his belief that each
megatrend renders the past obsolete and promises unlimited
progress for the future. He posits a straight line upward into
the Age of Information without regard for the wisdom of Ralph
Waldo Emerson who admitted, "Society never advances." Emerson was a realist, not a pessimist. He knew that every human
advancement has a trade-off by which we lose something of
value when we gain something else.

Whatever the reason behind the jubilant ending of Naisbitt's
book, it is a refreshing change from the pessimism of earlier
futurists. A book edited by Alvin Toffler, entitled *The Futurists,*
samples the key thoughts of the social critics, scientists, phi-
losophers and planners who gained identity as leaders of the

futurist movement in the 1960s and 1970s.[1] Their conclusions stand in stark contrast to Naisbitt's finale.

> It is the top of the ninth inning. Man, always a threat at the plate, has been hitting Nature hard. It is important to remember, however, that NATURE BATS LAST.
>
> — Paul Ehrlich

> We must place the future, like the unborn child in the womb of a woman, within a community of men, women, and children, already among us, already here, already to be nourished and succored and protected, already in need of things for which, if they are not prepared before it is born, it will be too late. So, as the young say, The Future Is Now.
>
> — Margaret Mead

> They (the young radicals) will be "the pain" in mankind's body. But this is only a hope; no certainty at all. Still the possibility of "evolution by unsuccessful revolutions" seems worth considering.
>
> — Robert Jungk

> Our first and most pressing need, therefore, before we can begin to gently guide our evolutionary destiny, before we can build a humane future, is to halt the runaway acceleration that is subjecting multitudes to the threat of future shock while, at the very same moment, intensifying all of the problems they must deal with — war, ecological incursions, racism, the obscene contrast between rich and poor, the revolt of the young, and the rise of a potentially deadly mass irrationalism.
>
> — Alvin Toffler

> How can a planner anticipate what will be "good" and "right" and "proper" tomorrow? . . . Their values may be too narrow. They are probably not values held by society as a whole. Perhaps worse, their values are today's values, not those which will

be held by people in the future. This is a form of
tyranny — the tyranny of the present.

If you make forecasts, be aware of this possibility.
                                        — Theodore J. Gordon

To sum up: The West has to settle for falling expectations; in the developing world we may do well to
go on supporting growing expectations up to the
point where the development threatens to become
counterproductive. And when the balance is reached,
we may, with some luck, congratulate ourselves on
having averted disaster. But until then we have a
hard row to hoe.
                                        — Eric Jantsch

Unless we at least make a beginning on a process
for solving the immediate problems we will not have
much chance at solving the larger ones. On the
other hand, it may also be true that a long-run
vision, as it were, of the deep crisis which faces
mankind may predispose people to taking more interest in the immediate problems and to devote more
effort for their solution. This may sound like a rather
modest optimism, but perhaps a modest optimism
is better than no optimism at all.
                                        — Kenneth Boulding

Real science . . . implies the existence of Potent
Man. Omnipotent matter, like the omnipotent God
of traditional religion, is a fantasy into which people
can retreat in order to escape the challenge of taking
themselves seriously as creative animals . . .

Recognition of this can give us the faith we need
to face the future. It is an intensely humanistic faith,
but not totally opposed to religion. Rather, it is a recovery of the prophetic faith which has always been
found at the core of the world's great religions, but
has hitherto been upheld by only a very small perse-
cuted minority.
                                        — John Wren-Lewis

> We can survive only by learning to operate in our
> universe in a very different way. If we do not com-
> prehend and behave spontaneously with the highest,
> most unselfish integrity, I think man may readily
> not make it on this particular planet.
>   — R. Buckminster Fuller

Note the words that reveal the philosophy of these prominent
futurists:

> evolutionary destiny
> community of men, women and children
> humanistic faith
> creative animals
> Potent Man

Note then the "tonal" words and phrases that follow their
evolutionary and humanistic philosophy:

> Nature bats last
> it will be too late
> the pain in mankind's body
> threat of future shock
> tyranny of the present
> falling expectations
> obscene
> deadly
> disaster

Only Kenneth Boulding, whom we have already recognized
as a creative thinker with respect for the Christian faith, dares
to speak the words "modest optimism." As he notes in the
book, *The Meaning of the Twentieth Century,* there is a direct
connection between our world view and our view of the world.[2]

Megatrends is a new breed of futurism. Naisbitt's technique
of projecting trends from a five-state sample of news reports
is less sophisticated than the statistically-calculated predictions
of the Club of Rome or even the scholarly-based information
of Toffler's works. His unbridled optimism, however, is a feature

which connects his belief in rising human consciousness with the hope of Americans in the 1980s. The fact that Naisbitt ignores the mounting despair of poor, ethnic and elderly people, the alarming evidence of moral breakdown, and the underlying dis-ease over our economic and nuclear future is a warning that his optimism is shallow and short-lived. To make a prediction about his predictions:

OPTIMISM BASED UPON THE INHERENT GOODNESS AND RISING CONSCIOUSNESS OF HUMAN NATURE WILL END IN PESSIMISM ABOUT OUR HUMAN FUTURE.

While futurists contribute to the mood swings of our society, their influence is overshadowed by the media. One moment, we share a wave of triumph as Christa McCauliffe walks into a space shuttle. Seconds later, our faces mirror the numbing shock of her parents who have just watched the shuttle explode.

One of the missing megatrends in Naisbitt's book is the effect of instant information upon our national mood. He foresees the action of Hi/Tech and the reaction of Hi/Touch, but Naisbitt only infers the emotional force of information in creating euphoria or despair, compassion or anger, togetherness or loneliness, exhilaration or exhaustion. If what we have seen as the dawning of the Age of Information is projected into the full daylight of the future, we realize that we are heading for emotional instability characterized by manic-depressive mood swings of psychotic proportions. In human personality, we know that emotions tend to balance each other out. Emotional highs are compensated by emotional lows, but not in extreme form in the healthy personality. If, however, emotions and energies are pushed to a fever pitch beyond the boundaries of a healthy response, the compensating swing is a lurch into depression and exhaustion.

Schizophrenia is a sick way of protecting the personality against unpleasant reality. By denying the real world with which one cannot cope, the personality is protected by fantasy and withdrawal.

How much information about the real world can we emotionally absorb without defending our national personality by withdrawal, denial and fantasy? How often can instant information jerk our emotions from manic highs to depressive lows without a breakdown of our national personality? These questions lead to the greater question that is yet unanswered:

WHO WILL SET THE BALANCING TONE
FOR OUR SOCIETY IN THE AGE OF INFORMATION?

Perhaps it is the inadequacy of our Christian world view that has caused us to fall into the pessimistic trap of secular futurists. One of my hidden desires is to conduct "man on the street" interviews across the nation and ask the question: What single, descriptive word comes to your mind when I mention the name "evangelical Christian"? My guess is that the responses would tend to be negative for those who were not of the faith. In press conferences and public meetings where the subject of evangelical Christianity is raised, the typical reaction is that we are:

> seeking political power;
> exercising social protest; and
> demanding special privileges.

If so, the "man on the street" sees us to be a rather peevish lot of people.

One of the most critical questions with which the church must deal during the closing years of the twentieth century is its new-found political power. Evangelical Christians, in particular, must ask whether or not its recent lurch from relative political isolation to wholesale political involvement is a reaction that may become counter-productive to its long-term witness. At best, we are neophytes in the political process and generally naive about the pitfalls of political involvement. Strange as it seems, with each new political alignment we lose a bit of our objectivity which is essential to prophetic proclamation and we move a step away from our primary identity as a spiritual rather than a political force. Strange as it seems, we fail to learn from the liberals whose theology is bankrupt because of political contamination.

Although we charge the media with giving evangelical Christianity a "bad press," we must also take responsibility for the image we create. Two editorial cartoons come to mind. One is a cartoon divided into four parts. In the upper left hand corner is a drawing of a Bible with a traditional two-pronged silk ribbon sticking out as a marker for the pages. Below the Bible is a copy of the United States Constitution. In the upper right-hand section, the ribbon turns into a snake with glaring eyes and a forked tongue. At the bottom left, the extended snake is shown biting into the Constitution, and in the final section, it pulls back into the Bible with a triumphant sneer and a bite of the Constitution in its mouth. However unfair the cartoon may be, it conveys a message to the general public which says Bible-believing Christians are against our Constitutional freedoms. I wanted to shout, "That's not my Bible or my belief."

The second cartoon came out at the same time that abortion clinics were being bombed and the Shroud of Turin was being analyzed by scientists. In one of the nation's most widely read newspapers, an abortion bomber was shown wearing a shroud which had the marks of the crucified Christ. The top of the shroud, however, had the eye holes of a mask and came to a peak. No doubt remained. Christians, abortion bombers and the Ku Klux Klan were portrayed as one and the same. Again, I wanted to cry out, "That's not my Christ or my attitude."

Under ordinary circumstances, the editors of these cartoons could be sued for libel. But the fact is that our political involvement in constitutional issues and moral problems has made evangelical Christians "fair game" in the public arena. If we can't stand the heat, we will have to get out of the kitchen. But something more than a "bad press" is at stake in our political forays.

WHAT TONE ARE WE CREATING
FOR THE MESSAGE OF THE GOSPEL?

Our contest for political power is joined by our protest against specific moral issues. We evangelical Christians are known for our selective protest against the symptoms of sin, but we are equally known for our silent consent for the systemics of sin. Of course, such a division is unfair because the line between personal and public morality cannot be clearly drawn. Yet, once again, we must ask about the impression we are creating in the public mind. If the man on the street described evangelical Christians by the word "protest," would he be right?

Protest is usually a reaction against a problem after it has become an issue of national concern. By reacting against moral epidemics of drugs, alcohol, gambling and pornography, evangelical Christians are always just behind a fast-moving moral front. Proactive and preventative action is almost unknown among us. Consequently, our effectiveness is reduced and our reputation for reaction is reinforced. Kenneth Kantzer, former editor of *Christianity Today,* indicts all of us when he notes that public morality has continued to decline during the past decade at the same time that evangelical Christians have risen in public popularity and political power. Is "reactionary" a term that the man on the street would use to characterize social action by evangelical Christians today?

With our power and protest has come the demand for special privileges. An agenda for national reform includes prayer in public schools, teaching of creationism in classrooms, equal access in public schools for religious groups, and tuition vouchers for students choosing private schools. While each case can be defended on the basis of the preservation of traditional values and the freedom to exercise our religion, there is also an underlying element of special privilege built into this agenda. Prayer in public schools is a case in point. Deep within our national consciousness is the debatable assumption that the United States is historically a Christian nation and that Christianity is still the favored faith. Therefore, even though the specific nature of prayer in the public schools cannot be sectarian, it is assumed

that the superiority of Christianity will prevail. Similar assumptions support each of the other agenda items mentioned above.
With popularity and power has come a sense of special privilege,
a residue of the civil religion which was debated and rejected
in the 1970s. One is reminded of the prejudicial adage which
was used to characterize the Roman Catholic Church in its
church-state relationships:

WHEN YOU ARE IN POWER,
WE DEMAND OUR RIGHTS,
WHEN WE ARE IN POWER, YOU HAVE NO RIGHTS.

Are evangelical Christians creating a similar prejudice in
public opinion by demanding privileges beyond our rights?
Would the man in the street add "arrogance" to his list of
words describing our public image?

If evangelical Christians are identified by the public as
power, protest and privilege, it means that we have failed to
communicate the good news of the gospel to our generation.

THE CHURCH IS THE TONE-SETTER
FOR OUR SOCIETY.

To this point, it appears as if the secular society has set
the tone for the church. Our problems look like its problems.
Our keynote echoes its keynote.

The time has come for the church to strike its own tone.
Lloyd Ogilvie, in his book *If God Cares, Why Do I Still Have
Problems?* tells a story about Lloyd Douglas, author of *The
Magnificent Obsession* and *The Robe.*[3] Douglas enjoyed visiting
an old violin teacher who lived in a shabby setting but always
had a word of good news. One morning, Douglas stopped to
see him and asked, "Well, what's the good news today?"

Putting down his violin, the man stepped over to a tuning
fork suspended from a silk cord. He struck it a sharp blow
with a padded mallet and said, "There's the good news for
today. That, my friend, was an *A*. It was an *A* all day yesterday.

It will be an *A* all day tomorrow, next week and for a thousand years."

The church has a tone to strike against which all other instruments of the society must be tuned. It is an *A* that does not vary with the changing of society or the passing of civilizations.

JOY IS THE KEYNOTE OF THE CHRISTIAN IN EVERY GENERATION.

Joy is the clear, pure note of the Christian which will still be heard over the mush and meaninglessness of the Information Age. To sound that clarion note, however, we need to understand what Christ meant when He prayed that our "joy might be full."

To begin, we must dispel the notion that "joy" is just another human emotion on a scale ranging from pleasure to bliss through happiness, joy and gladness. On this scale, joy is a vivid, profound, demonstrative and intense, but transcient emotion which is less shallow than happiness, less serene than gladness, and less perfect than bliss. If, however, we read the biblical meaning of joy as communicated by Jesus, it is a quality of life with a tone of its own.

The joy of Christ is informational. Perhaps we will be surprised to learn that the joy of Christ is always related to information. In John 17:13, Jesus prays to His Father,

> And now I come to thee; and these things I speak
> in the world, that they may have my joy fulfilled
> in themselves.

Throughout the Scriptures, the Word of God and the quality of joy cannot be separated. If the good news and the joyful sound are disconnected, irreparable damage is done to the truth and the tone of the gospel.

Evangelical is a strong biblical term that is synonymous with the good news of the gospel and unites Hi/Truth with Hi/Tone. By definition, *good news* means a divine fusion between textual integrity and tonal quality. In the Age of Information, the tendency will be to battle on textual grounds in order to preserve the truth. But, as we have already seen in the inerrancy debate, the warfare turns inward and the truth becomes fodder for a theological civil war. Joy also can be turned inward in self-serving enthusiasm but not without becoming part of the noise of a thousand mushy voices. *Good News* is exclusively an outgoing message with a transcending tone. Therefore, every Christian is called to be an evangelical in the full biblical sense of the word.

THE JOY OF CHRIST IS AN INTRINSIC QUALITY.

Human emotions are induced by external circumstance. *Happiness* for instance, is a word rooted in the "hap" of chance or good luck. Accordingly, happiness rises and falls with the circumstances of life. Joy is just the opposite. It is an intrinsic quality which is independent of circumstances. Jesus gives us the secret of His joy when He speaks about abiding in the love of His Father (John 15:9-11). As C. S. Lewis discovered in his search for joy, it is never an end or object in itself, but ever and always the by-product of a relationship with God who is our "overwhelming First." *By-product* is too incidental a word. Paul writes to the Galatians that joy is a fruit of the Spirit (Galatians 5:22). The analogy of fruit confirms the intrinsic quality of joy — not a gift to be given, but a quality to be known — as natural to the Spirit-filled life as the fruit is to the tree.

THE JOY OF CHRIST IS INTEGRATIVE.

To classify joy as another emotion is to miss the larger meaning of the experience that Christ knew.

> *Cognitively,* joy is a fact related to knowing the Word of God;

> *affectively,* joy is a feeling related to experiencing the presence of God; and

volitionally, joy is a decision related to obeying the commandments of God.

Joy, then, is an attribute of Christian character which goes deeper, but does not deny, our emotions and goes beyond, but does not reject, our environment. In personality theory, joy qualifies as a "source trait" of Christian character which is pervasively and spontaneously expressed in the "surface traits" of our attitudes and behavior. In other words, joy is a quality of life that cannot be faked.

THE JOY OF CHRIST IS SACRAMENTAL.

Through the sacrament of the Lord's Supper, we Christians celebrate life in the midst of death. Joy is an expression of that life in Christ. How else can we account for the fact that joy is linked in Scripture with:

> persecution (Acts 5:41);
> imprisonment (Acts 16:25);
> sorrow (2 Corinthians 6:10); and
> suffering (1 Peter 4:12,13).

Even greater mystery surrounds the closing moments in Jesus' life as the reality of His passion falls like a black shroud upon His soul. Instead of succumbing to the despair of death, the note of joy picks up tempo and rises in pitch through His words. Whereas joy is mentioned just once in the Gospel of John during the early years of Jesus' ministry, suddenly it becomes the dominant theme of His prayers and promises as He approaches the cross. Why? Is it not the knowledge that He will finish His work and return to His Father? Hebrews 12:2 takes on new meaning as we read:

> Who for the joy that was set before him endured
> the cross, despising the shame, and is set down at
> the right hand of the throne of God.

Mystery of mysteries! Joy increases with suffering and overflows under the threat of death, not because of some kind of spiritual masochism, but in the knowledge of being faithful to the very end. Christ's first words to the women at the tomb, after His resurrection, are, "Joy to you." Only Christians can know the full meaning of that greeting. Life in the midst of death is our sacrament of joy.

SELF-INTEREST IS THE KILLER OF JOY.

One theme defines the quality of joy — obedience to the Word and will of God. Suddenly, we know why the note of joy has been muffled in our generation. The same insidious influence of self-interest that has put conditions on our commitment to God has compromised our obedience to His Word and robbed us of our joy. Consequently, we who confess the name of Christ and profess to be "evangelicals" are better known for the jealous protection of our privileges than we are for the joyful expression of our faith.

In Alan Paton's novel, *Ah, But Your Land Is Beautiful,* Nhlapo, the headmaster of a school for blacks, compromises on his principles in order to preserve his pension. Trouble clouds his soul as he realizes that he has forsaken his people. Seeking out his best friend as a counselor, Nhlapo says, "The jolly, laughing man is gone. I'm not sure that he will ever come back."[4]

Christian joy is equally dependent upon our integrity to the Word and the will of God. If our obedience is compromised by self-interest, our note of joy rings like a cracked bell. The jolly, laughing man is gone.

In the foreword to his book, *Jesus Rediscovered,* Malcolm Muggeridge tells about traveling to the Holy Land to make films on the New Testament for BBC television. As he filmed the series, he realized that many of the shrines and legends of the Christian faith are fraudulent. But then he saw a party of Christian pilgrims at one of the shrines, "their faces bright with faith, their voices, as they sang, so evidently and joyously aware of the Savior's nearness." He could only confess, "I was conscious of His presence."[5]

PRAISE IS THE CORPORATE TONE
FOR THE CHURCH IN THE AGE OF INFORMATION.

Praise is the corporate expression of personal joy. Acts profiles the post-Pentecostal church. Preoccupied with that church's program for effective evangelism, we may miss the tonal quality of its witness in the world. Acts 2:46,47 (NKJV) reads:

> And continuing daily with one accord in the temple, and breaking bread from house to house, they ate their food with *gladness* and *simplicity of heart, praising God* and having *favor* with all the people. And the Lord added to the church daily those who were being saved.

"And" serves as a holy conjunction in a sequence of cause and effect. "Praising God" is the *stimulus;* "having favor with all the people" is the *response;* and the Lord adding "to the church daily those who were being saved" is the *result.* A climate conducive to redemption is created by the church "praising God." Like joy, praise is a Christian quality that the world does not fault. In fact, the whole world slumps when the church turns from praise to protest. Even pagans join in with the church celebrating Christmas and Easter. Rather than complaining about the commercialism of these holidays, the church, through them, can show a secular society how to celebrate. As a young Yuppie described the morning after a secular night's pleasure, "It is ashes in the mouth and dirty bedsheets."

In contrast, one Monday, after Easter Sunday, the morning newspaper featured a four-color picture on the front page showing Christians at a sunrise service in a local park. The air was filled with multi-colored balloons and the sunrise worshippers were watching them soar upward from their outstretched hands. It looked like opening day at the races until I read the caption. On each balloon was printed the message:

CHRIST IS RISEN, ALLELUJAH!

This was no hot-air celebration. Children for miles around would scramble for those balloons, take them home and ask their parents to read the names and tell them what they meant. A safe prediction is that sometime in the future a convert to Christianity will tell about a balloon, released in celebration, that first carried the good news to a child's heart.

The celebrating church must never get away from the object of its praise. Notably, the early church made its reputation in the world by "praising God." Celebrations can easily be turned into ends in themselves. Sometimes our preparations for praise are so elaborate that the performance itself becomes the object of glory. On the other hand, sometimes our preparations for praise are so sloppy that God must be embarrassed. Constant attention must be given to assure that God is the object of praise and that His glory is our goal.

Mass communication via electronic media is an ideal means through which the church can celebrate and praise God. To the credit of gospel TV, praise is an integral part of its message. The problem is that the words and songs tend to be limited to a Christian audience, and are broadcast in the language and to the tunes of the Christian subculture. For praise to be effective in creating a climate conducive to redemption, it must be the tone above tones, projected to the masses and resonating with their needs. Imagine the impact of a Christian festival of praise carried over the secular media which was specifically programmed for the needs of non-believers.

Some years ago, Moral Rearmament had an exercise for its college students who were preparing to take the message of the movement to those who had never heard its story. The students were instructed to imagine themselves on a barge floating down a river in a foreign land. Native peoples crowded to river banks as the barge passed by. The students were given this assignment: "You have just five minutes to tell your story. What would you show and tell the people in five minutes to convince them that your story is true?" Not by coincidence,

Moral Rearmament chose to communicate its message world-wide through the singing voices and dancing feet of handsome young people who exemplified the theme, "Up With People."

Anticipating the Age of Information, the church needs to ask the same question: If we had just five minutes to communicate the gospel to the masses, what would we show and tell? The work of the Holy Spirit in the early church has already given us the answer. We would want to show and tell the church praising God by singing,

> **Praise the Lord, praise the Lord,**
> Let the earth hear His voice!
> **Praise the Lord, praise the Lord,**
> Let the people rejoice!
> O come to the Father,
> Thru Jesus the Son,
> And give Him the glory,
> **Great things He hath done.**

CONCLUSION

16.

A Tract for Our Times

Imagine that you are a traveler along an English road in the eighteenth century. Coming toward you is a lone rider. His reins are slack, and his eyes are riveted on a book. As he comes closer, you recognize the dimunitive man who shook and saved England through the power of the Spirit of God. John Wesley is the rider. Back and forth across England he rode, more than 250,000 miles on horseback, reading and writing as he went.

John Wesley carried his library and his desk in saddlebags on the back of his horse. I have often wished that I could have rummaged through those saddlebags. In addition to his Bible, Wesley carried a commentary, a devotional book, a literary classic, his own medical manual, manuscripts for his sermons, correspondence with his preachers, music for his flute, and many tracts which he had written on the issues of the day. Wesley was a Renaissance man in his own time and in his own way.

In Wesley's saddlebags was a curriculum for living in a time of parenthesis between eras of human civilization. At the core of the curriculum was the Word of God. Wesley said it for us, "I am a man of one Book." The Scriptures were his field guide for the future. Obedient to the Spirit of Truth, Wesley did prophetic mapwork for eighteenth-century England. Under the teaching of the same Spirit, he read widely in the fields of human learning. In his day as well as ours, there was the danger of separating Christian faith from human knowledge. His brother Charles prayed:

> Let us unite these two,
> So long divided,
> Learning and vital piety.

Few know that Wesley's inquisitive and creative mind took him into the fields of medicine and music. In the long and tedious miles between towns, you can imagine him alternating his reading with interludes of music on the flute.

The tracts in his saddlebags are equally instructive for us. To Wesley, they represented the speediest information system for his age. Of course, "information float" between the sender and receiver involved days, not seconds as we know today. When a social issue or a spiritual concern came to Wesley's attention, he wrote a tract which could be quickly published and distributed to influence the direction of Christian response. Tracts served as a medium by which Wesley could give a timely response to the new information of the eighteenth century.

IN THE COMING AGE OF INFORMATION, TIMELY TRACTS WILL COME BACK INTO STYLE.

Each day, we are being caught by surprise as new information with moral and spiritual implications comes to us through the media. Concise and current statements are the most effective means for a quick response to issues which, through the media, catch us by surprise, rise to a peak, and then give way to another surprise. Wesley's tracts will no longer suffice. He had time to write, print and circulate his tracts before the issue was resolved. We do not. In our time of parenthesis, we are rapidly losing the luxury of submitting our moral and spiritual dilemmas to a long and labored theologial research. Nor can we continue to react emotionally to fast-moving issues that go past us and do not allow us to catch up. Our thinking as Christians must undergo the dramatic shift from *reaction* to *anticipation* for our Christian response to moral and spiritual issues in our time.

The moral and spiritual future is not unlike our defense against nuclear attack. Norbert Weiner, in the book, *God and Golem,* recalls the time when surprise was a limited weapon in warfare.[1] Pearl Harbor is an example. The Japanese struck us by surprise, but lacked the will or the weapons for the knockout blow. Consequently, the United States gained the time to marshal our forces and avoid defeat. Nuclear weapons take away the advantage of reaction time. As Weiner notes, once the nuclear missile is launched, we are seconds away from total destruction. Even an alleged "fail-safe" system may be faulty. Therefore, the whole context of warfare is changed from a defensive reaction to an anticipatory strategy that includes the "first strike" potential.

Moral and spiritual issues in the Age of Information will come at us like multiple warheads from nuclear missiles. Our defensive reaction will be too slow and our "fail-safe" theologies may prove faulty. We will have no choice but to think strategically and respond proactively. Even now, we need evangelical "think tanks" in which Christian scholars and practitioners anticipate the pending and the possible in order to issue "ethical impact" statements for positioning on future issues.

Within the recent past, the need for strategic Christian thinking has come to us in frightening form. While the debate over abortion boils over in legislative halls and courtrooms and on the streets, a new wonder drug is announced that will serve as a birth control or "morning-after pill" with no side effects. In contrast with current birth control pills which block fertilization of the egg, this new pill stops the fertilized egg from implantation in the wall of the uterus. A woman taking the drug will never know when or if she has spontaneously aborted a baby. Gone is the trauma of decision-making in reaction to the news of pregnancy. Only the anticipatory decision remains.

Does a woman choose to take a pill which would abort a fertilized egg even if she never knows when fertilization has taken place?

On the other side of the life spectrum, the Judicial Committee of the American Medical Association recommended that no unusual means, including water and food, be given to prolong the life of a comatose patient. A court ruling has extended that recommendation to terminally-ill patients, comatose or not.

Pro-life advocates are quick to point out the fact that their worst fears are being realized. Once we cheapen the value of life at the beginning, they say, it is only a matter of time before we cheapen life at the end.

If only the issue were that simple! We have yet to face the fact that medical science is advancing by quantum leaps that cannot be stopped, avoided or ignored. In the accelerating Age of Information, almost every moral assumption upon which we have relied for answers to life-and-death questions will be severely tested. We may react, but we will not put a halt to the inevitable march of medicine. Then, having reacted in theory, we will acquiesce in practice.

Our changing attitude toward divorce is an example. At first, we responded to the new statistics with reactionary answers, and held to "biblical grounds" as the only justification for marital breakup. But then divorce struck our family, our friends and our church leaders. Amazing theological adjustments took place. Today, we accept divorce as a regrettable, but forgiveable, fact of life on situational grounds. Even "no-fault" divorce on grounds of "irreconcilable differences" has become accepted among us.

If the pattern persists, we will see the day when the names "abortion" and "euthanasia" will be changed so that the reality of our decision-making in matters of life and death can be justified. Our alternative is to shift from reactionary to anticipatory biblical ethics. Not all of our moral dilemmas will be solved, but at least we will become known for our reflection as well as our reaction.

At its best, *MegaTruth* is a tract which calls upon Christians to anticipate the issues of the Age of Information. If it achieves its goal, clergy and laity will begin to ask, "Lord, what do You want me to do?" A thousand questions have been raised and fingers are pointed in the direction of the answers. More important is the attitude that we bring to the Age of Information. As Naisbitt suggests, we may become like dinosaurs waiting for the weather to change. Or, we may claim Christ's promise that He will send us the Spirit of Truth as our guide and our gyroscope for living in the coming age. Most important, then, will be that we bring the Spirit to our search and discovery mission during this time of parenthesis. We cannot accept Naisbitt's open-ended shout based upon evolutionary theory and humanistic theology, "My God, what a fantastic time to be alive!" Neither are we ready to give up on the world before God does.

WE HAVE A STORY TO TELL.

A fable for the Age of Information begins with a man asking a computer, "Will you ever think like a man?"

Disks whirr, lights blink and the computer answers, "Let me tell you a story."

Story-telling is distinctive to our human nature. A story is the essence of the Christian message. In the incarnation, death and resurrection of Jesus Christ, all human history comes together with meaning, morality and hope. Therefore, to conclude our search and discovery mission for *MegaTruth in the Age of Information,* let me tell you a story.

As a junior high school student I quaked through the hell-fire, brimstone and end-time preaching of revivals and camp meetings. Life lost its joy and work lost its meaning as I disciplined my behavior, despised the world and denied the future. Spiritual neurosis set in. Just when I should have been living life to its fullest, I suffered under a burden of fear that I would not be ready for the rapture. Then one day our English teacher read to us Whittier's narrative poem entitled, "Abraham Davenport."

On May 19, 1780, a "horror of great darkness" fell over New England at midday. Men prayed and women wept as they listened for the "doom blast of the trumpet" and looked for the "dreadful face of Christ." In the old State House of Connecticut, the lawgivers trembled and said, "It is the Lord's Great Day! Let us adjourn." But then Abraham Davenport rose to speak. Cleaving the "intolerable hush" with a steady voice, he said,

> This well may be
> The Day of Judgment which the world awaits;
> But be it so or not, I only know
> My present duty, and my Lord's command
> To occupy till He come. So at the post
> Where He set me in His providence,
> I choose, for one, to meet Him face to face,
> No faithless servant frightened from my task,
> But ready when the Lord of harvest calls;
> And therefore, with all reverence, I would say,
> Let God do His work, we will see to ours,
> *Bring in the candles.*

Then, straight to the issue and with a dry natural sense of humor, Abraham Davenport debated an amendment to an act regulating shad and alewife fisheries!

> And there he stands in memory to this day,
> Erect, self-poised, a rugged face, half seen
> Against the background of unnatural dark,
> A witness to the ages as they pass,
> *That simple duty hath no place for fear.*

I was set free — to live faithfully to the past, fully in the present, and freely for the future. You will understand then why I anticipate the coming Age of Information. I see the Church of Jesus Christ:

discovering the full meaning of Christ's promise to give us the Spirit of Truth;

discerning the signs of the times and the trends of tomorrow through the teaching of the Spirit;

offering the Christian world view as the only meaningful, moral and hopeful alternative to the dead-end views of secularism, scientism and humanism;

leading the way out of our "time of parenthesis" through the spiritual renewal and social reform of a Great Awakening;

engaging truth through the experience and presence of the Spirit of Truth;

extending our relationships in self-giving love to bring outsiders into Christ with us;

exercising our stewardship for economic resources to serve the "poor" among us;

creating cooperative networks for fulfilling the preaching, baptizing and teaching functions for world evangelization;

empowering the laity for effective ministry through the focused vision, meaningful communication, trustworthy positioning and self-deployment of leaders with a sense of self-worth; and

setting the tone of Christ's joy as the keynote for our society.

BRING IN THE CANDLES!

How should *MegaTruth* end? My natural enthusiasm resonates with John Naisbitt's shout, "My God, what a fantastic time to be alive!" My spiritual understanding is in tune with Hal Lindsey's prayer, "Maranatha — Even so, Lord Jesus, come quickly." My love for doing the work of God concurs with Christ's command, "Occupy till I come." My heart sings out the melody of our Lord's first words to the women at the tomb after the resurrection, "Joy to you!" My hope for the future leans forward to grasp Christ's on-going promise, "Behold, I make all things new."

While trying to choose among these options for an ending, the Spirit of Truth opened my eyes to the meaning of MegaTruth for an information-based society. With the "Ah, ha!" of a new discovery, I see that the Great Commission (Matthew 28:18-20) anticipates the Age of Information.

For the *power of information,* Jesus reminds us,

> ALL *POWER* IS GIVEN UNTO ME IN HEAVEN
> AND IN EARTH (KJV).

For the *potential of information systems,* Jesus commands us,

> *GO* THEREFORE AND MAKE DISCIPLES OF
> ALL THE NATIONS, *BAPTIZING* THEM IN THE
> NAME OF THE FATHER AND THE SON AND
> THE HOLY SPIRIT, *TEACHING* THEM TO OB-
> SERVE ALL THAT I COMMANDED YOU (NASB).

For the *peril and promise of the coming Age of Information,* Jesus assures us,

> LO, I AM WITH YOU ALWAYS, EVEN TO THE
> END OF THE AGE (NASB).

Amen.

SO BE IT, LORD!

Notes

Chapter 1
1. John Naisbitt, *Megatrends* (New York: Warner Books, 1982).
2. Ibid., p. 249.
3. Hal Lindsey, *The Late Great Planet Earth* (Grand Rapids, Michigan: Zondervan, 1970), p. 188.

Chapter 2
1. John Naisbitt, *Megatrends* (New York: Warner Books, 1982), p.6.
2. Ibid., p. 3.
3. Ibid., p. 4.
4. Herman Kahn and Anthony J. Wiener, *The Year Two Thousand* (New York: MacMillan, 1967), pp. 6-13.
5. Daniel Yankelovich, *New Rules: Living in a World Turned Upside Down* (New York: Random House, 1981), pp. xii-xx.

Chapter 3
1. Christopher Lasch, *The Culture of Narcissism* (New York: W. Norton & Co., 1978).
2. Robert Ringer, *Looking Out for Number One* (New York: Funk & Wagnalls, 1977).
3. Amitai Etzioni, *An Immodest Agenda* (New York: McGraw-Hill, 1982), p. 3.
4. William G. McLoughlin, *Revivals, Awakenings, and Reform* (Chicago: University of Chicago Press, 1978), pp. 12-16.

Chapter 4
1. John Naisbitt, *Megatrends* (New York: Warner Books, 1982), p. 24.

Chapter 5

1. C. S. Lewis, *The Screwtape Letters* (New York: MacMillan, rev. paperback ed. 1982), p. 10.
2. Francis Schaeffer, *The Christian Manifesto* (Westchester, Illinois: Crossway Books, 1981), p. 117.
3. Franky Schaeffer, *A Time for Anger* (Westchester, Illinois: Crossway Books, 1982), p. 54.
4. Richard Quebedeaux, *The Worldly Evangelicals* (San Francisco: Harper & Row, 1978).
5. George Gallup, Jr., *The Search for America's Faith* (Nashville: Abingdon, 1980), p. 89.
6. Ibid., pp. 122-23.
7. Harry Blamires, *Where Do We Stand?* (Ann Arbor, Michigan: Servant Books, 1980), p. 4.
8. Kenneth Boulding, *The Meaning of the Twentieth Century: The Great Transition* (New York: Harper Colophon Books, 1965), pp. 162-63.

Chapter 6

1. Gordon Allport, *The Individual and His Religion* (New York: Macmillan, 1962), pp. 76-81.
2. Harry Blamires, *Where Do We Stand?* (Ann Arbor, Michigan: Servant Books, 1980), p. 59.
3. James Orr, *The Christian View of God and the World* (Grand Rapids, Michigan: William B. Eerdmans, 1954), pp. 32-34.
4. Harry Blamires, *The Christian Mind* (Ann Arbor, Michigan: Servant Books, 1978).
5. B. F. Skinner, *Walden Two* (New York: Macmillan, paperback ed., 1962), p. 320.
6. George Orwell, *Nineteen Eighty-Four* (New York: New American Library, Signet Classics, 1971).

Chapter 7

1. Quoted in *Agenda for Theology,* by Thomas C. Oden (San Francisco: Harper & Row, 1979), pp. 111-12.
2. Robert C. Roberts, "Therapy for the Saints," *Christianity Today* (November 8, 1985), p. 25.

Chapter 8
1. Jacques Ellul, *The Meaning of the City* (Grand Rapids, Michigan: William B. Eerdmans, 1970), pp. 181-82.

Chapter 9
1. Parker Palmer, *To Know As We Are Known/A Spirituality of Education* (San Francisco: Harper & Row, 1983), pp. 22-24.
2. Ibid., p. 31.

Chapter 10
1. Herman Kahn and Anthony J. Wiener, *The Year Two Thousand* (New York: Macmillan, 1968), pp. 341-45.
2. Daniel Yankelovich, *New Rules: Living in a World Turned Upside Down* (New York: Random House, 1981), pp. 4-5.
3. Abraham H. Maslow, *Motivation and Personality* (New York: Harper & Row, 1954), pp. 80-106.
4. Lawrence Kohlberg, "Stages of Moral Development as a Basis for Moral Education," eds. Clive Beck, et. al., *Moral Education* (Toronto: University of Toronto Press, 1970), pp. 23-92. See also Kohlberg's *Philosopy of Moral Development* (San Francisco: Harper & Row, 1981), pp. 118-22.
5. C. S. Lewis, *The Four Loves* (New York: Harcourt Brace and World, 1960), p. 177.
6. James Earl Massey, "The Coloring of America," *Christianity Today* (January 17, 1986), p. 11-I.
7. H. Newton Moloney, "The Graying of America," *Christianity Today* (January 17, 1986), pp. 8-I to 9-I.
8. Massey, "Coloring of America," p. 11-I.
9. Ibid.

Chapter 11
1. Quoted in *The Search for America's Faith* by George Gallup, Jr., and David Poling (Nashville: Abingdon, 1980), p. 123.
2. James Earl Massey, "Coloring of America," *Christianity Today* (January 17, 1986), p. 10-I.
3. John Naisbitt, *Megatrends* (New York: Warner Books, 1982), p. 57.
4. Neil Chesanow, *The World-Class Executive* (New York: Rawson Associates, 1985).

5. Studs Terkel, *Working* (New York: Pantheon Books, 1972), Intro. p. xxiv.

Chapter 12

1. George Cabot Lodge, *The New American Ideology* (New York: Alfred A. Knoph, 1975), p. 160.
2. John Naisbitt, *Megatrends* (New York: Warner Books, 1982), p. 97.
3. Terrence E. Deal and Allan A. Kennedy, *Corporate Cultures* (Reading, Massachusetts: Addison-Wesley, 1982), pp. 182-83.
4. Thomas J. Peters and Robert H. Waterman, Jr., *In Search of Excellence* (New York: Warner Books, 1982), p. 277.
5. Benjamin B. Tregoe and John W. Zimmerman, *Top Management Strategy: What It Is and How To Make It Work* (New York: Simon & Schuster, 1980), p. 17.

Chapter 13

1. Peter Drucker, *The Effective Executive* (New York: Harper & Row, 1967), pp. 15-16.
2. Richard N. Ostling, "Power, Glory, and Politics," *Time* (February 17, 1986), pp. 62-63.

Chapter 14

1. Warren Bennis and Burt Nanus, *Leaders: Strategies for Taking Charge* (New York: Harper & Row, 1985).
2. Robert Townsend, *Up the Organization* (New York: Alfred A. Knopf, 1970), p. 110.
3. Bennis and Nanus, *Leaders,* pp. 58-60.
4. Ibid., pp. 79-84.
5. Ted Engstrom and Ed Dayton, *Christian Leadership,* (April, 1986).

Chapter 15

1. Alvin Toffler, ed., *The Futurists* (New York: Random House, 1972). This source is divided into sections, each one by the indicated author. Page numbers of the quotes are: Ehrlich, p. 26; Mead, p. 50; Jungk, p. 84; Toffler, p. 130; Gordon,

p. 189; Jantsch, p. 232; Boulding, pp. 242-43; Wren-Lewis, pp. 296-97; Fuller, p. 306.
2. Kenneth Boulding, *The Meaning of the Twentieth Century: The Great Transition* (New York: Harper Colophon Books, 1965), p. 163.
3. Lloyd J. Ogilvie, *If God Cares, Why Do I Still Have Problems?* (Waco, Texas: Word Books, 1985), p. 166.
4. Alan Paton, *Ah, But Your Land Is Beautiful* (New York: Charles Scribner's Sons, 1981), p. 51.
5. Malcolm Muggeridge, *Jesus Rediscovered* (New York: Doubleday, 1969), Foreword, pp. x-xi.

Chapter 16
1. Norbert Weiner, *God and Golem* (London: Chapman & Hall, 1964), pp. 66-69.

Bibliography

Bennis, Warren and Nanus, Burt. *Leaders: Strategies for Taking Charge*. New York: Harper & Row, 1985.

Blamires, Harry. *The Christian Mind*. Ann Arbor, Michigan: Servant Books, 1978.

_____ . *Where Do We Stand?* Ann Arbor, Michigan: Servant Books, 1980.

Boulding, Kenneth. *The Meaning of the Twentieth Century: The Great Transition*. New York: Harper Colophon Books, 1965.

Chesanow, Neil. *The World-Class Executive*. New York: Rawson Associates, 1985.

Deal, Terrence E. and Kennedy, Allan A. *Corporate Cultures*. Reading, Massachusetts: Addison-Wesley, 1982.

Drucker, Peter. *The Effective Executive*. New York: Harper & Row, 1967.

Ellul, Jaques. *The Meaning of the City*. Grand Rapids, Michigan: William B. Eerdmans, 1970.

Gallup, George, Jr., and Poling, David. *The Search for America's Faith*. Nashville: Abingdon, 1980.

Kahn, Herman and Wiener, Anthony J. *The Year Two Thousand*. New York: Macmillan, 1968.

Lasch, Christopher. *The Culture of Narcissism*. New York: W. W. Norton & Co., 1978.

Lewis, C. S. *The Screwtape Letters*. New York: Macmillan, revised paperback edition, 1982.

_____ . *The Four Loves*. New York: Harcourt Brace Jovanovich, 1971.

Lindsey, Hal. *The Late Great Planet Earth*. Grand Rapids, Michigan: Zondervan, 1970.

Muggeridge, Malcolm. *Jesus Rediscovered*. New York: Doubleday, 1969.

Naisbitt, John. *Megatrends*. New York: Warner Books, 1982.

Oden, Thomas C. *Agenda for Theology*. San Francisco: Harper & Row, 1979.

209

Palmer, Parker J. *To Know As We Are Known/A Spirituality of Education*. San Francisco: Harper & Row, 1983.

Peters, Thomas J. and Waterman, Robert H., Jr. *In Search of Excellence*. New York: Warner Books, 1982.

Quebedeaux, Richard. *The Worldly Evangelicals*. San Francisco: Harper & Row, 1978.

Schaeffer, Francis. *A Christian Manifesto*. Westchester, Illinois: Crossway Books, 1981.

Schaeffer, Franky. *A Time for Anger: The Myth of Neutrality*. Westchester, Illinois: Crossway Books, 1982.

Seamands, David A. *Healing for Damaged Emotions*. Wheaton, Illinois: Victor Books, 1981.

Toffler, Alvin. *Future Shock*. New York: Random House, 1970.

——————————— . *The Futurists*. New York: Random House, 1972.

——————————— . *The Third Wave*. New York: Bantam Books, 1981.

Tregoe, Benjamin B. and Zimmerman, John W. *Top Management Strategy: What It Is and How to Make It Work*. New York: Simon & Schuster, 1980.

Weiner, Norbert. *God and Golem*. London: Chapman & Hall, 1964.

Yankelovich, Daniel. *New Rules: Living In a World Turned Upside Down*. New York: Random House, 1981.